Communications
in Computer and Information Science 1747

More information about this series at https://link.springer.com/bookseries/7899

Abderrahmane Nitaj · Karim Zkik (Eds.)

Cryptography, Codes and Cyber Security

First International Conference, I4CS 2022
Casablanca, Morocco, October 27–28, 2022
Proceedings

Editors
Abderrahmane Nitaj 🆔
University of Caen Normandy
Caen, France

Karim Zkik
ESAIP
Angers, France

ISSN 1865-0929   ISSN 1865-0937 (electronic)
Communications in Computer and Information Science
ISBN 978-3-031-23200-8   ISBN 978-3-031-23201-5 (eBook)
https://doi.org/10.1007/978-3-031-23201-5

This Springer imprint is published by the registered company Springer Nature Switzerland AG
The registered company address is: Gewerbestrasse 11, 6330 Cham, Switzerland

Preface

This volume contains the papers accepted for presentation at I4CS 2022, the first International Conference on Cryptology, Coding Theory and Cyber Security. The aim of I4CS is to provide an international forum for researchers and practitioners from academia and industry from all over the world to present and discuss all forms of cryptography and coding theory and their applications, specifically in cybersecurity. I4CS 2022 was held in Casablanca, Morocco, during October 27–28, 2022, on the initiative of the organizers from Ben M'sick Faculty of Sciences, Hassan II University, Casablanca, in cooperation with the International Association for Cryptologic Research (IACR).

The contents of the volume consists of three full invited papers and four contributed papers. In total, 12 papers were submitted. The Technical Program Committee was composed of 18 members and two external reviewers, and decided to accept four papers. All submitted papers received three reviews in a double-blind process. We are grateful to the members of the Program Committee and the external reviewers for their work.

We heartily thank the authors of all submitted papers for their interest in the conference. The authors of accepted papers were given a week to revise and prepare their papers according to the suggestions of the reviewers. The revised versions of the accepted papers were not checked again by the Program Committee, so authors bear full responsibility for their content. The president of the Hassan II University of Casablanca, the Dean of the Ben M'sick Faculty of Sciences, Mhammed Talbi, and the General Chair, Khadija Bouzkoura, as well as the local Organizing Committee deployed a great effort in the planning phase of the conference. We are also thankful to the staff at Springer for their help with producing the proceedings and to the staff of EasyChair for the use of their conference management system.

October 2022

Abderrahmane Nitaj
Karim Zkik

Organization

I4CS 2022 was organized by Hassan II University of Casablanca, Morocco, in cooperation with the International Association for Cryptologic Research (IACR).

General Chair

Khadija Bouzkoura — Hassan II University, Casablanca, Morocco

Program Chairs

Abderrahmane Nitaj — University of Caen Normandie, France
Karim Zkik — ESAIP, Angers, France

Organizing Committee

Khadija Bouzkoura (Chair) — Hassan II University, Casablanca, Morocco
Mohamed Azouazi — Hassan II University, Casablanca, Morocco
Hassan Laarabi — Hassan II University, Casablanca, Morocco
El Houssine Labriji — Hassan II University, Casablanca, Morocco
Abderrahim Tragha — Hassan II University, Casablanca, Morocco
Abdelhakim Chillali — Sidi Mohamed Ben Abdullah University, Taza, Morocco
Mohamed Abdou Elomary — Hassan I University, Settat, Morocco

Program Committee

Muhammad Rezal Kamel Ariffin — Universiti Putra Malaysia, Malaysia
François Arnaud — University of Limoges, France
Daniele Bartoli — University of Perugia, Italy
Florian Caullery — Qualcomm, France
Pierre-Louis Cayrel — University of Saint-Etienne, France
Pierre-Louis Cayrel — University of Saint-Etienne, France
Luca DeFeo — IBM Research Zürich, Switzerland
Pierre Dusart — University of Limoges, France
Philippe Gaborit — University of Limoges, France
Elisa Gorla — University of Neuchatel, Switzerland
Kenza Guenda — USTHB, Algeria
Cheikh Thiecoumba Gueye — Universite Cheikh Anta Diop, Senegal
Sylvain Guilley — Télécom Paris and CNRS, France
Delaram Kahrobaei — The City University of New York, USA

Juliane Krämer	University of Regensburg, Germany
Abderrahmane Nitaj	LMNO, University of Caen Normandie, France
Ferruh Ozbudak	Middle East Technical University, Ankara, Turkey
Palash Sarkar	Indian Statistical Institute, Kolkata, India
Amr Youssef	Concordia University, Canada

Additional Reviewers

Marzio Mula
Karl Southern

Invited Papers

Cryptanalysis of a Code-Based IdentificationScheme Presented in CANS 2018

Boly Seck[1,2] , Pierre-Louis Cayrel[2] , Idy Diop[1] ,
and Morgan Barbier[3]

[1] École Supérieure Polytechnique (ESP) de Dakar, Laboratoire D'imagerie
Médicale et de Bioinformatique, Dakar, Sénégal
seck.boly@ugb.edu.sn

[2] Univ Lyon, UJM-Saint-Etienne, CNRS, Laboratoire Hubert Curien UMR 5516,
F-42023, Saint-Etienne, France
pierre.louis.cayrel@univ-st-etienne.fr

[3] ENSICAEN, Groupe de Recherche en Informatique et Instrumentation de Caen,
CNRS, Boulevard Maréchal Juin 14 000, Caen, France
morgan.barbier@ensicaen.fr

Abstract. NIST recently published the first four winning algorithms from the post-quantum cryptography (PQC) standardization process that has been ongoing since 2017. The four algorithms selected are a key establishment algorithm called CRYSTALS-Kyber and three digital signature algorithms called CRYSTALS-Dilithium, FALCON, and SPHINCS+. The first two of these signature schemes are based on structured lattices and the last is a hash-based signature scheme. These future standards will be the default options for post-quantum algorithm selection in most security products. To diversify post-quantum signature standards, NIST has issued a call for submissions for signature schemes that have short signatures and fast verification before June 1, 2023. Code-based signatures schemes are promising candidates for this additional process. In this paper, we first show that the rank-based Veron's identification scheme proposed in [6] in CANS 2018 reveals information in the response step. Second, we perform an attack on the support of the error to find the secret in this scheme. Finally, we propose a secure zero-knowledge identification protocol with rank settings and a code-based signature scheme with fast verification.

Keywords: NIST PQC standardization· Code-based signature· Cryptanalysis· Rank metric

An Embedded AI-Based Smart IntrusionDetection System for Edge-to-Cloud Systems

Ritu-Ranjan Shrivastwa⬤, Zakaria Bouakka, Thomas Perianin,
Fabrice Dislaire, Tristan Gaudron, Youssef Souissi, Khaled Karray,
and Sylvain Guilley⬤

Secure-IC S.A.S., 15 Rue Claude Chappe Bât. B, 35510, Cesson-Sévigné,
France
ritu-ranjan.shrivastwa@secure-ic.com, zakaria.
bouakka@secure-ic.com, thomas.perianin@secure-ic.com,
fabrice.dislaire@secure-ic.com, tristan.gaudron@se-
cure-ic.com, youssef.souissi@secure-ic.com, khaled.kar-
ray@secure-ic.com, sylvain.guilley@secure-ic.com
https://www.secure-ic.com/

Abstract. This article proposes a general purpose IoT framework usually applicable to all Edge-to-Cloud applications and provides an evaluation study on a use-case involving automotive V2X architecture, tested and verified on a toy smart-car in an emulated smart-car environment. The architecture in study is finely tuned to mimic actual scenarios and therefore the sensors available on the toy car encompasses almost all the sensors that assist a regular ADAS in smart cars of today. The cloud connectivity is maintained through the CoAP protocol which is a standard IoT connectivity protocol. Finally, the security solution proposed is that of a smart Intrusion Detection System (IDS) that is built using Machine Learning (ML) technique and is deployed on the edge. The edge IDS is capable of performing anomaly detection and reporting both detection results as well as sensor collected big data to the cloud. On the cloud side the server stores and maintains the collected data for further retraining of ML models for edge anomaly detection which is differentiated into two categories viz. sensor anomaly detection model and network anomaly detection model. To demonstrate Software update Over The Air (SW-OTA) the cloud in the evaluation setup implements a ML model upgrade capability from the cloud to the connected edge. This implementation and evaluation provides a Proof-of-Concept of the choice of ML as IDS candidate and the framework in general to be applicable to various other IoT scenarios such as Healthcare, Smart-home, Smart-city, Harbour and Industrial environments, and so on, and paves way for future optimization studies.

Keywords: Edge computing · Artificial intelligence · Cybersecurity services · Embedded security · Anomaly detection · Intrusion detection systems · V2X · Internet of Things · Advanced Driver Assistance Systems (ADAS)

A New Addition Law in Twisted Edwards Curves on Non Local Ring

Moha Ben Taleb Elhamam[1] ⓘ, Abdelhakim Chillali[2] ⓘ,
and Lhoussain El Fadil[1] ⓘ

[1] Sidi Mohamed Ben Abdellah University, FSDM, Fez, Morocco
mohaelhomam@gmail.com, lhouelfadil2@gmail.com
[2] Sidi Mohamed Ben Abdellah University, FP, LSI, Taza, Morocco
abdelhakim.chillali@usmba.ac.ma

Abstract. Let $\mathbb{F}_q$ be a finite field of q elements with $q = p^r$ for some odd prime integer p and a positive integer r. Let $R = \mathbb{F}_q[e]$, where $e^2 = e$. The purpose of this paper is to investigate $E_{E,a,d}(R)$ be the twisted Edwards curves over R, with $a, d \in R$. In the end of the paper, we study the complexity of this new addition law in $E_{E,a,d}(R)$ and highlight some links of our results with elliptic curves cryptosystem.

Keywords. Twisted edwards curves · Addition law · Cryptography

Contributed Papers

New Lattice-Based Signature Based on Fiat-Shamir Framework Without Aborts

Chik How Tan and Theo Fanuela Prabowo

Temasek Laboratories, National University of Singapore, Singapore
tsltch@nus.edu.sg, tsltfp@nus.edu.sg

Abstract. Recently, a number of side-channel attacks were launched on lattice-based signatures based on "Fiat-Shamir with aborts". This shows that signature based on Fiat-Shamir with aborts is vulnerable to side-channel attacks. In this paper, we construct a lattice-based signature scheme based on Fiat-Shamir framework without aborts, and instantiate it over NTRU lattices. The proposed signature is proved to be secure in the random oracle model under some newly defined problems. We also prove the hardness of these new problems and show that the search RLWE problem is as hard as these newly defined problems. The public key size, secret key size and signature size of the proposed signature scheme are 1920 bytes, 512 bytes and 4096 bytes respectively for 180-bit quantum security level. The key and signature sizes of the proposed signature are comparable to those of the currently known signatures, such as, Dilithium, Falcon, qTESLA, MLS, BCM and MITAKA.

A Complementary Result on the Construction of Quadratic Cyclotomic Classes

Kamil Otal[1] and Eda Tekin[2]

[1] TÜBİTAK BİLGEM UEKAE, Gebze, Kocaeli, Türkiye
kamil.otal@gmail.com
[2] Karabük University, Karabük, Türkiye
tedatekin@gmail.com

Abstract. Side-channel analysis (SCA) is a general name for cryptanalytic methods based on side information gathered by measuring and analyzing of various physical parameters. Threshold implementation (TI) is one of the successful countermeasure techniques for some types of SCA. Within this scope, Nikova et al. gave an algorithm on the decomposition of power permutations into quadratic power permutations over finite fields $\mathbb{F}_{2^n}$ in [Cryptogr. Commun. 11, 37–384 (2019)]. Later on, Otal and Tekin gave a sufficient way in [Cryptogr. Commun. 13, 837-845 (2021)] to reduce the precomputation cost in the algorithm of Nikova et al. substantially. In this paper, we prove that this sufficient way is also necessary, in other words, the proposed way is an optimal solution. In that way, we provide a complementary result on the construction of quadratic cyclotomic classes.

Keywords: Boolean functions · S-boxes · Power permutations

A Framework for the Design of Secure and Efficient Proofs of Retrievability

Françoise Levy-dit-Vehel[1] and Maxime Roméas[2]

[1] LIX, ENSTA Paris, INRIA, Institut Polytechnique de Paris, 91120 Palaiseau,
France
levy@ensta.fr
[2] LIX, École polytechnique, INRIA, Institut Polytechnique de Paris, 91120
Palaiseau, France
romeas@lix.polytechnique.fr

Abstract. Proofs of Retrievability (PoR) protocols ensure that a client can fully retrieve a large outsourced file from an untrusted server. Good PoRs should have low communication complexity, small storage overhead and clear security guarantees with tight security bounds. The focus of this work is to design good PoR schemes with simple security proofs. To this end, we propose a framework for the design of secure and efficient PoR schemes that is based on Locally Correctable Codes, and whose security is phrased in the Constructive Cryptography model by Maurer. We give a first instantiation of our framework using the high rate lifted codes introduced by Guo et al. This yields an infinite family of good PoRs. We assert their security by solving a finite geometry problem, giving an explicit formula for the probability of an adversary to fool the client. Moreover, we show that the security of a PoR of Lavauzelle and Levy-dit-Vehel was overestimated and propose new secure parameters for it. Finally, using the local correctability properties of Tanner codes, we get another instantiation of our framework and derive an analogous formula for the success probability of the audit.

Compression Point in Field of Characteristic 3

Ismail Assoujaa⦿, Siham Ezzouak, and Hakima Mouanis

University Sidi Mohammed Ben Abdellah FSDM (labo: LASMA) Fez, Morocco
ismail.assoujja@usmba.ac.ma, siham.ezzouak@usmba.ac.
ma, hmouanis@yahoo.fr

Abstract. For some applications, systems and devices, it might be desirable to take as few as possible of bit memory space and still keep the same result. Compression point is a new method that used some arithmetic operation in (ECC) elliptic curve cryptography to reduce memory space. If we take any point on the elliptic curve, we can see that this point is consisting of two coordinates x and y, so with compression point we can compressed this point and keep only one coordinate x or y and one sign bit/trit, requiring only half the space. In this paper, we will show new methods of compression point that can save 25% of the space memory in fields of characteristic 3, and compare it with previous result.

Keywords. Elliptic curve · Compression point · Affine coordinate · Field of characteristic 3

Contents

Invited Papers

Cryptanalysis of a Code-Based Identification Scheme Presented in CANS 2018

Boly Seck[1,2(✉)] [iD], Pierre-Louis Cayrel[2] [iD], Idy Diop[1] [iD], and Morgan Barbier[3]

[1] Laboratoire d'imagerie médicale et de bioinformatique,
École Supérieure Polytechnique (ESP) de Dakar, Dakar, Senegal
seck.boly@ugb.edu.sn

[2] Univ Lyon, UJM-Saint-Etienne, CNRS, Laboratoire Hubert Curien UMR 5516,
42023 Saint-Etienne, France
pierre.louis.cayrel@univ-st-etienne.fr

[3] ENSICAEN, Groupe de recherche en informatique et instrumentation de Caen,
CNRS, Boulevard Maréchal Juin 14 000, Caen, France
morgan.barbier@ensicaen.fr

Abstract. NIST recently published the first four winning algorithms from the post-quantum cryptography (PQC) standardization process that has been ongoing since 2017. The four algorithms selected are a key establishment algorithm called CRYSTALS-Kyber and three digital signature algorithms called CRYSTALS-Dilithium, FALCON, and SPHINCS+. The first two of these signature schemes are based on structured lattices and the last is a hash-based signature scheme. These future standards will be the default options for post-quantum algorithm selection in most security products. To diversify post-quantum signature standards, NIST has issued a call for submissions for signature schemes that have short signatures and fast verification before June 1, 2023. Code-based signatures schemes are promising candidates for this additional process. In this paper, we first show that the rank-based Veron's identification scheme proposed in [6] in CANS 2018 reveals information in the response step. Second, we perform an attack on the support of the error to find the secret in this scheme. Finally, we propose a secure zero-knowledge identification protocol with rank settings and a code-based signature scheme with fast verification.

Keywords: NIST PQC standardization · Code-based signature · Cryptanalysis · Rank metric

1 Introduction

Over the past four decades, public key cryptography has become a cornerstone of our digital communication systems. In an increasingly connected world in the age of the Internet of Things, it has become more important than ever for individuals, businesses, and governments to communicate securely. Identification protocols are essential to the security of computer networks and smart cards. A zero-knowledge protocol is an interactive protocol where we prove knowledge about something without revealing any information about that knowledge. It is a useful tool for proving that a protocol can be reused without loss of security. Most practical zero-knowledge protocols are based on number theory, and it is worth looking for alternatives for at least two reasons: First, number theory-based schemes are often costly in terms of computational complexity, and second, Shor has shown in [40] that there are quantum algorithms that can solve the difficult problems of integer factorization and discrete logarithm. It was therefore crucial to develop cryptosystems that are resistant to quantum attacks. Thus, the NIST PQC has given a significant boost to research in post-quantum cryptography. The main goal of the process, which began in 2017, is to replace three standards that are considered particularly vulnerable to quantum attacks, namely public key encryption, key establishment, and digital signature.

On July 5, 2022, NIST published the first four winning algorithms, three of which are signature schemes. CRYSTALS -Dilithium [34] is a signature scheme from identification scheme using Fiat- Shamir with aborts. Its security can be reduced to the security of the module learning with errors (MLWE) and module short integer solution (MSIS) problems. It is designed to allow fast multiplications using the NTT transformation and avoids generation of randomness from a discrete Gaussian distribution. FALCON [23] is a signature scheme whose design is based on the Gentry-Peikert-Vaikuntanathan (GPV) blueprint [52] for lattice-based signatures using trapdoor functions. FALCON is constructed using NTRU lattices and is designed to compute all arithmetic operations using Fourier-transform techniques. SPHINCS+ [10] is a framework that describes a family of hash-based signature schemes. Unlike other signature schemes that require a hard-to-solve mathematical problem, the general concept of building signature schemes from hash functions goes back to the beginning of public-key cryptography [30]. As a result, SPHINCS+ is widely considered to be the most conservative security signature scheme. The code-based signature is a promising candidate for the additional NIST PQC standardization process for digital signature.

The idea of using error-correcting codes to build an identification algorithm comes from Harari [27] and Stern's scheme, which was the first identification scheme based on the syndrome decoding (SD) problem [42]. Unlike McEliece's public-key encryption scheme [36] or the signature scheme of Courtois, Finiasz, and Sendrier (CFS) [18], Stern's scheme uses a random binary matrix in the Hamming metric, meaning that there is no trap in it. Therefore, other identification schemes in the Hamming metric have been proposed. The identification scheme of Véron [43], unlike the other schemes based on the SD problem, defines a dual version of Stern using a generator matrix of a random linear binary code. In [14], Cayrel, Véron, and El Yousfi propose a zero-knowledge identification scheme called CVE based on the q-ary SD problem. Unfortunately, most of these schemes are impractical, with the major drawback being the large signature size. In [3] Baldi *et al.* introduce a new variant of the SD problem called the Restricted Syndrome Decoding (R- SD) problem, where the entries of the searched vector are defined over a subset of the underlying finite field. They describe how zero-knowledge identification schemes based on the SD problem can be modified to be based on the R- SD problem. They show that this leads to compact public keys as well as significantly reduced communication costs. The original idea of code-based cryptography is not tied to the choice of metric and is adapted for other metrics.

In response, Chen proposed [17] an efficient zero-knowledge identification protocol in the spirit of Shamir's Permuted Kernel Problem (PKP) [21] without using a hash function and based on the Syndrome Decoding problem in the rank metric (RSD). This problem is less known and less studied than in the case of the Hamming metric but it is believed to be hard by the community. After two attacks proposed in [15] and [37], the Chen zero-knowledge identification protocol is completely broken by Gaborit *et al.* in [26]. The two attacks proposed in this paper are made possible by the fact that the zero-knowledge proof of the Chen protocol is flawed. The first attack relies on an unsatisfactory way to hide the secret vector by simple right-hand matrix multiplication. The second attack exploits the non-use of a hash function in the commitment step. In the end, they propose a new zero-knowledge identification scheme in rank metric. Therefore, all zero-knowledge identification schemes in Hamming metric can be adapted to rank metric. However, the rank-based Veron's protocol presented in [6] in CANS 2018 leaks information in the response step.

Contribution. In this paper, we first found an information leak in the rank-based Véron identification protocol proposed in [6] before breaking it with an error support attack. The attack relies on an unsatisfactory way to mask the secret error vector e by a simple permutation over $\mathbb{F}_{q^m}^n$. Second, we present a zero-knowledge rank-based Véron identification protocol with the rank-metric settings. Finally, we propose an efficient code-based signature scheme in rank metric.

Organisation. The paper is organized as follows. Sections 2 and 3 recall the basic facts on the rank metric and the rank-based Véron identification protocol proposed by Bellini *et al.*. In Sect. 4, we show the weak masking of the secret in their protocol and how to break it with low complexity. In Sect. 5, we propose a repaired version of the identification scheme with rank metric parameters. Section 6 presents our efficient code-based signature scheme and finally, we conclude this paper in Sect. 7.

2   Notation and Definitions for Rank-Based Cryptography

Gabidulin introduced the rank metric into code theory in 1985 [24]. The complexity of generic decoding in the rank metric is exponential and more difficult than in the Hamming metric for the same parameters. Codes in the rank metric have been variously proposed as alternatives to error-correcting codes in cryptography. We refer the reader to Loidreau's paper [33] for more details on the rank metric and its applications in cryptography.

2.1   Notation

Let q be a power of a prime p, m an integer, and let x be an n-dimensional vector space over the finite field $\mathbb{F}_{q^m}$. Let $\beta_1, \ldots, \beta_m$ be a basis of $\mathbb{F}_{q^m}$ over $\mathbb{F}_q$. To each vector $x \in \mathbb{F}_{q^m}^n$ we can associate a matrix M_x.

$$x = (x_1, \ldots, x_n) \in \mathbb{F}_{q^m}^n \to M_x = \begin{pmatrix} x_{1,1} & \cdots & x_{n,1} \\ \vdots & & \vdots \\ x_{1,m} & \cdots & x_{n,m} \end{pmatrix} \in \mathbb{F}_q^{m \times n} \tag{1}$$

such that $x_i = \sum_{j=1}^{m} x_{ij}\beta_j$ for each $i \in \{1, \ldots, n\}$. The rank weight of a vector x is defined as the rank of the associated matrix M_x. We have $\mathbf{r}(x) = \mathbf{r}(M_x)$ and the rank metric between two vectors x, y is given by $\mathrm{dr}(x, y) = \mathbf{r}(M_x - M_y)$.

2.2   Definitions

Definition 1 (Support of a word). *Let* $x = (x_1, \ldots, x_n) \in \mathbb{F}_{q^m}^n$. *The support* E *of* x *is the* $\mathbb{F}_q$-*subspace of* $\mathbb{F}_{q^m}$ *generated by the coordinates of* x:

$$E = \langle x_1, \ldots, x_n \rangle_{\mathbb{F}_q}$$

The weight of a word is equal to the dimension of support. The number $\mathbb{F}_q$-vector subspaces of dimension w in $\mathbb{F}_{q^m}$ is denoted by the Gaussian coefficient $\begin{bmatrix} m \\ w \end{bmatrix}_q$ and is equal to [32]:

$$\begin{bmatrix} m \\ w \end{bmatrix}_q = \prod_{i=0}^{w-1} \frac{q^m - q^i}{q^w - q^i} \approx q^{w(m-w)}.$$

Definition 2 (Special permutation). *Let* $x = (x_1, \ldots, x_n) \in \mathbb{F}_{q^m}^n$ *of rank weight* $r(x) = w$ *and support* E. *Let* $\Sigma \in S_n$ *be a permutation and an* $(m \times m)$-*matrix* Γ *(*$\Gamma_{i,j} \neq 0$, $i = 1, \ldots, n$ *and* $j = 1, \ldots, m$*) of rank weight* w. *We define the transformation* $\Pi_{\Gamma,\Sigma}$ *as:*

$\Pi_{\Gamma,\Sigma} : \mathbb{F}_{q^m}^n \longrightarrow \mathbb{F}_{q^m}^n$
$(x_1, \ldots, x_n) \longmapsto (\Gamma_{1,1}x_{1,\Sigma(1)} + \ldots + \Gamma_{1,m}x_{m,\Sigma(1)} \cdots \Gamma_{m,1}x_{1,\Sigma(n)} + \ldots + \Gamma_{m,m}x_{m,\Sigma(n)})$

The formula to compute the function $\Pi_{\Gamma,\Sigma}(x)$ *is as follows:*

$$\Pi_{\Gamma,\Sigma}(x) := \Sigma \left(\begin{pmatrix} \Gamma_{1,1} & \cdots & \Gamma_{1,m} \\ \vdots & & \vdots \\ \Gamma_{m,1} & \cdots & \Gamma_{m,m} \end{pmatrix} \begin{pmatrix} x_{1,1} & \cdots & x_{1,n} \\ \vdots & & \vdots \\ x_{m,1} & \cdots & x_{m,n} \end{pmatrix} \right)$$

$$= \begin{pmatrix} \Gamma_{1,1}x_{1,\Sigma(1)} + \ldots + \Gamma_{1,m}x_{m,\Sigma(1)} & \cdots & \Gamma_{1,1}x_{1\Sigma(n)} + \ldots + \Gamma_{1,m}x_{m\Sigma(n)} \\ \vdots & \ddots & \vdots \\ \Gamma_{m,1}x_{1\Sigma(1)} + \ldots + \Gamma_{m,m}x_{m,\Sigma(1)} & \cdots & \Gamma_{m,1}x_{1\Sigma(n)} + \ldots + \Gamma_{m,m}x_{m,\Sigma(n)} \end{pmatrix} \in \mathbb{F}_q^{m \times n}$$

Notice that $r(\Pi_{\Gamma,\Sigma}(x)) = r(x) = \dim(E) = w$.

This function has the property of preserving the rank of a vector in $\mathbb{F}_{q^m}^n$. We use Γ for the linear transformation and Σ for the coordinate permutation. This definition can be generalized as in [26]. This transformation has improved the security of some schemes presented in CANS [5] and [7].

Definition 3 (Syndrome Decoding (SD) problem). *Let $H \in \mathbb{F}_q^{(n-k)\times n}$ be a parity-check matrix of an $[n, k]$ code over $\mathbb{F}_q$, $s \in \mathbb{F}_q^{n-k}$ and t an integer. The SD problem is to find $e \in \mathbb{F}_q^n$ such that $He^T = s$ and $wt(e) \leq t$, where wt denotes the Hamming weight.*

The SD problem was proven $\mathcal{NP}$-hard in [8]. This problem can be naturally extended in the case of the rank metric.

Definition 4 (Syndrome Decoding problem in the rank metric (RSD)). *Let the parity-check matrix $H \in \mathbb{F}_{q^m}^{(n-k)\times n}$, $s \in \mathbb{F}_{q^m}^{n-k}$ and w an integer. The RSD problem is to find $e \in \mathbb{F}_{q^m}^n$ such that $He^T = s$ and $r(e) = w$, where r denotes the rank weight.*

Definition 5 (Small-weight codeword problem). *Let $\mathcal{C}$ be an $[n, k]$ code and w an integer. The problem consists to find a codeword $c \in \mathcal{C}$ such that $r(c) = w$.*

2.3 Rank-Based Cryptography

The security of the rank-based Véron protocol is based on the syndrome decoding problem in the rank metric. We first recall here the SD problem in the Hamming metric.

Syndrome Decoding problem. The most efficient generic attack against code-based cryptosystems like the McEliece encryption scheme, the CFS signature scheme, and others is the Information Set Decoding (ISD) approach [39]. The original algorithm of ISD starts from the received word $y = xG + e$ and consists of guessing a set of k coordinates of y with no error (an information set). If we find this set with probability $\frac{\binom{n-t}{k}}{\binom{n}{k}}$, we will do a linear inversion of a $k \times k$ matrix to recover x.

Another approach consists of starting from the syndrome Hy^T of length $n - k$. The idea is in guessing a set of $n - k$ coordinates which contains the support of the error e with probability $\frac{\binom{n-t}{n-k-t}}{\binom{n}{n-k}}$, it is possible to recover the error e by an $(n - k) \times (n - k)$ matrix inversion from the syndrome of the message.

The first classical ISD algorithm in Hamming metric is proposed by Prange in [39] followed by a series of improvements in [4, 11, 12, 20, 22, 35, 38, 41].

Syndrome Decoding Problem in the Rank Metric. The analog of ISD attack in the Hamming metric is how to randomly choose information sets and check if the respective coordinates are the error support. The main improvement is how to cleverly choose the information set. To recover the support, the naive approach is to try all possible supports *i.e.* all vector spaces of dimension w before solving a system. This is the Chabaud-Stern [15] attack with $q^{w(m-w)}$ bases to enumerate. The attack is improved by Ourivski and Johannson in [37] and the number of bases is now less than $(k + w)^3 q^{(w-1)(m-w)+2}$. The algorithm proposed by Gaborit *et al.* in [25] improves the support attacks in $\min(\mathcal{O}((n - k)^3 m^3 q^{w\lceil \frac{km}{n} \rceil}), \mathcal{O}((n - k)^3 m^3 q^{(w-1)\lceil \frac{(k+1)m}{n} \rceil}))$. Thereafter, Aragon *et al.* [2] proposed a new algorithm that gives the support attack in $\mathcal{O}((n - k)^3 m^3 q^{w\lceil \frac{(k+1)m}{n} \rceil - m})$.

2.4   The Algorithm of Gaborit, Ruatta, and Schreck (GRS)

The general idea to solve the RSD problem is to find an overspace E' such that $E \subset E'$. Then we can express the coordinates of x on the basis of E' and solve the linear system given by the parity-check equations.

Let $\mathcal{C}$ be an $[n, k]$ random code over $\mathbb{F}_{q^m}$ with generator matrix $G \in \mathbb{F}_{q^m}^{k \times n}$ and suppose we receive $y = c + e$ for $c \in \mathcal{C}$ and $\mathbf{r}(e) = w$, in particular for $e = (e_1, \ldots, e_n)$ there exists a subspace E of dimension w which contains all the errors coordinates e_i. If we denote by $(E_1, \ldots, E_w)$ a basis of E, we get $e_{i,j} \in \mathbb{F}_q (1 \le i \le n, \ 1 \le j \le w)$ such that

$$e_i = \sum_{j=1}^{w} e_{i,j} E_{i,j} \tag{2}$$

Let H be a matrix of the dual code of $\mathcal{C}$. Then the parity equations are:

$$He^T = Hy^T. \tag{3}$$

Suppose now we know a subspace E' of dimension $w' \ge w$ which contains E, then for all e_i, we denote $(E'_1, \ldots, E'_{w'})$ a basis of E', there exist $e'_{i,j} \in \mathbb{F}_q$ such that

$$e_i = \sum_{j=1}^{w} e'_{i,j} E'_{i,j}.$$

Hence we obtain nw' unknowns. The number of syndrome equations (3) over $\mathbb{F}_q$ is $(n - k) \times m$ and it is possible to recover e_i by solving a linear system, as long as, $nw' \le (n - k) \times m$; and hence:

$$w' \le \left\lfloor \frac{(n - k)m}{n} \right\rfloor = m + \left\lfloor \frac{-km}{n} \right\rfloor \tag{4}$$

Now we find the probability that $E \subset E'$.

Suppose that E' is fixed. The number of choices for E is the number of vector subspaces of dimension w in a space of dimension m with coefficients in $\mathbb{F}_q$, is

$\begin{bmatrix} m \\ w \end{bmatrix}_q$. The number of favorable cases is equal to the number of vector subspaces of E' of dimension w' (it is necessary that E is either one of them), is $\begin{bmatrix} w' & w \end{bmatrix}'_q$. Thus we have:

$$\mathbb{P}(E \subset E') = \frac{\begin{bmatrix} w' \\ w \end{bmatrix}_q}{\begin{bmatrix} m \\ w \end{bmatrix}_q} \approx \frac{q^{w(w'-w)}}{q^{w(m-w)}} = q^{-w(m-w')} \tag{5}$$

Hence if we take $w' = m + \lfloor \frac{-km}{n} \rfloor$ we obtain a probability that E is included in a random space E' of dimension w', which is $q^{-w(m-w')} = q^{w\lceil \frac{km}{n} \rceil}$. Therefore, if we also take into account the complexity of the matrix inversion, we obtain the complexity below:

$$\mathcal{O}\left((n-k)^3 m^3 q^{w\lceil \frac{km}{n} \rceil} \right) \tag{6}$$

Let us consider the subspace $e^{-1}E$ of dimension w containing the vector 1. We apply the same method as before, but the dimension of the code is $k+1$ and we know one element of E. The number of syndrome equations over $\mathbb{F}_q$ is $(n-k-1) \times m$. Therefore, the dimension w' of E' must satisfy:

$$w' = m + \left\lfloor \frac{-(k+1)m}{n} \right\rfloor \tag{7}$$

Remark: this algorithm is also a search algorithm for small-weight words in random code.

The probability that $e^{-1}E \subset E'$ is therefore

$$\mathbb{P}(e^{-1}E \subset E') = \frac{\begin{bmatrix} w' \\ w-1 \end{bmatrix}_q}{\begin{bmatrix} m \\ w-1 \end{bmatrix}_q} \approx q^{-(w-1)(m-w')} \tag{8}$$

Since we know that $1 \in E$, we just need that the remaining $w-1$ elements of a basis of E are also in E', which gives a probability $q^{(w-1)\lceil \frac{(k+1)m}{n} \rceil}$. Once we recover $e^{-1}E$, taking e^{-1} as unknown in syndrome equations permits us to recover it at almost no cost. Overall if we add the polynomial complexity we get:

$$\mathcal{O}\left((n-k)^3 m^3 q^{(w-1)\lceil \frac{(k+1)m}{n} \rceil} \right) \tag{9}$$

It is important to note that knowledge of more than one vector of the basis of E allows the improvement of this algorithm.

Prover		Verifier
sk, pk $= (x, e), (y, G, w)$		pk

$u \leftarrow\!\!\$\ \mathbb{F}_{q^m}^k,\ \sigma \leftarrow\!\!\$\ S_n$

$c_1 \leftarrow \mathtt{hash}(\sigma)$

$c_2 \leftarrow \mathtt{hash}(\sigma(u+x) \cdot G)$

$c_3 \leftarrow \mathtt{hash}(\sigma(u \cdot G + y))$ $\qquad \xrightarrow{\ c_1, c_2, c_3\ }$

$\qquad\qquad\qquad\qquad\quad \xleftarrow{\quad b \quad}$ $\qquad b \leftarrow\!\!\$\ \{0, 1, 2\}$

if $b = 0$

$\qquad$ if $c_1 = \mathtt{hash}(\mathrm{rsp}_1)$ and

$\qquad \mathrm{rsp}_1 \leftarrow \sigma$ $\qquad \xrightarrow{\ \mathrm{rsp}_1, \mathrm{rsp}_2\ }$ $\qquad\quad c_2 = \mathtt{hash}(\mathrm{rsp}_1(\mathrm{rsp}_2 \cdot G))$

$\qquad \mathrm{rsp}_2 \leftarrow u + x$

$\qquad\qquad\qquad\qquad\qquad\qquad\qquad$ **return true**

if $b = 1$

$\qquad$ if $c_2 = \mathtt{hash}(\mathrm{rsp}_1)$ and

$\qquad \mathrm{rsp}_1 \leftarrow \sigma((u+x) \cdot G)$ $\qquad \xrightarrow{\ \mathrm{rsp}_1, \mathrm{rsp}_2\ }$ $\qquad\quad c_3 = \mathtt{hash}(\mathrm{rsp}_1 + \mathrm{rsp}_2)$

$\qquad \mathrm{rsp}_2 \leftarrow \sigma(e)$ $\qquad\qquad\qquad\qquad\qquad$ and $\mathbf{r}(\mathrm{rsp}_2) = w$

$\qquad\qquad\qquad\qquad\qquad\qquad\qquad$ **return true**

if $b = 2$

$\qquad$ if $c_1 = \mathtt{hash}(\mathrm{rsp}_1)$ and

$\qquad \mathrm{rsp}_1 \leftarrow \sigma$ $\qquad \xrightarrow{\ \mathrm{rsp}_1, \mathrm{rsp}_2\ }$ $\qquad\quad c_3 = \mathtt{hash}(\mathrm{rsp}_1(\mathrm{rsp}_2 \cdot G + y))$

$\qquad \mathrm{rsp}_2 \leftarrow u$

$\qquad\qquad\qquad\qquad\qquad\qquad\qquad$ **return true**

Fig. 1. Rank-based Véron's identification protocol in [6]

3   The Protocol Proposed by Bellini *et al.*

In this section, we describe the protocol presented in [6]. They instantiate the Véron identification protocol (from [43]) in rank-metric settings.

The Véron identification protocol is a 3-pass zero-knowledge protocol with a cheating probability of $\frac{2}{3}$. The scheme uses a random $(n \times k)$ matrix G over $\mathbb{F}_{q^m}$ as the generator matrix of a random linear code. The context is as follows:

Common Public Data: G a generator matrix and $\mathtt{hash}$ a hash function,
Secret Key: $x \in \mathbb{F}_{q^m}^k$ and $e \in \mathbb{F}_{q^m}^n$,
Public Key: $y = xG + e$ and $\mathbf{r}(e) = w$.

Alice (**the prover**) knows the solution e of the SD $\mathcal{NP}$-complete problem. Bob (**the verifier**) asks Alice a series of questions. If Alice knows e, she can answer all the questions correctly. If she does not, she has a probability q of answering correctly. After δ successful rounds of the protocol, Bob will be convinced that Alice knows e with a probability of $1 - q^\delta$.

The crucial point of this protocol is to make good masking of the secret e i.e., to transform e with a given rank weight w into any other word with the same weight. But in implementing the protocol, Bellini *et al.* use a permutation σ in $\mathbb{F}_{q^m}$ Fig. 1. This is not sufficient to properly mask e, so this scheme is not zero-knowledge and leaks information during the response step. The properties of this scheme are given in Table 1 (h is the output size of the hash function).

Table 1. Properties of identification protocol in [6]

Size of the matrix in bits	$m \times k \times n$
Size of the public identification	$mn + \log_2(w)$
Size of the secret key	$mk + mn$
Total number of bits exchanged	$\delta(3h + 2 + \frac{2}{3}(n + m(k + n)))$

4 Cryptanalysis

In this section, we highlight the flaw in the zero-knowledge proof of the previous protocol and use the GRS algorithm to recover the e secret. We need only to access the public data exchanged during the protocol to recover the secret. The hiding of the secret e in step 4 (Fig. 1, $b = 1$) by a simple permutation in $\mathbb{F}_{q^m}$ is weak and leaks information.

4.1 Flaws in Rank-Based Véron protocol

Recall that this attack on the support of e has been used in other scenarios such as in [26] and [31]. In the protocol in [6], a random permutation σ is used to mask the private vector e into a potential secret $\sigma(e)$ of rank w. However, this reveals the non-zero values of the vector while keeping their positions secret. This information is useless when binary codes are used, but it gives the attacker an advantage when the codes belong to $\mathbb{F}_{q^m}^n$. So, masking the secret by σ is weak and leaks information. In addition, in the case of Stern's protocol, a permutation of coordinates over $\mathbb{F}_{2^m}$ has the property that it can transform any codeword with a given Hamming weight into any codeword with the same weight. This point is crucial for indistinguishability in the zero-knowledge proof. In the case of this protocol, the permutation is not the equivalent notion to that of the permutation for the Hamming distance. The permutation $\sigma(e)$ permits to change of coordinate positions of e but not the support of e. So, the coordinates of $\sigma(e)$ and e generate the same vector space E over $\mathbb{F}_q$. To break this scheme we apply the GRS algorithm.

4.2   Our Attack and Result

In the interactive protocol, the prover wants each time to prove the knowledge of e without revealing any information about it. The attack presented here takes place in step 4 ($b = 1$) in the description of the protocol (Fig. 1). This is the time during which the prover must send $\sigma(e)$. The attack uses the fact that the support of e can be recovered from $\sigma(e)$ with low complexity.

In this scenario, the attack avoids the exponential search of basis as in [15]. We generate a basis of w vectors and express each coordinate e_i of e into this basis as in Sect. 2.4. We construct a basis $(E_1, \ldots, E_w, E_{w+1}, \ldots, E_m)$ of $\mathbb{F}_{q^m}$ over $\mathbb{F}_q$ and write the syndrome equation (3) with this basis. We obtain $(n - k) \times m$ equations on $\mathbb{F}_q$ and $n \times w$ unknowns. Thus the GRS algorithm is reduced to the resolution of a linear system. The parameters proposed $(q = 2, n = 64, w = 9, k = 30, m = 80)$ in [6] permit to solve directly the system by Gaussian elimination for recovering the secret e. The cost of this attack in this case for all parameters proposed in [6] is a Gaussian elimination for a matrix of size $(n - k) \times m$.

This attack was performed on an Intel® Core™ i7-7700 CPU running at 3.60×8 GHz, having 32 GB of RAM, and running a 64-bit version of Ubuntu 18.04.5 LTS. The runtime results with the proposed parameters in [6] are presented in Table 2.

Table 2. Runtime of our attack.

Variant	n	m	w	k	Time (ms)
Véron80	35	48	5	16	14
Véron128	64	80	9	30	26

5   New Identification Scheme

We propose a new protocol for which correct zero-knowledge proof is possible. It implies in particular the use of correct masking (using a special permutation of definition 2). Masking the secret e by a random permutation $\sigma(e)$ is replaced by $\Pi_{\Gamma, \Sigma}(e)$ as summarized in Fig. 2.

We recall that the cost of a complete interaction between the two parties is the number of bits exchanged. In Steps 3 and 5 (Fig. 2, $b = 0$ and $b = 2$) of our identification scheme (or repaired rank-based Véron's identification), the prover sends ℓ_Σ bits (where $\ell_\Sigma < n$) and ℓ_Γ bits (where $\ell_\Gamma < m$). These are the seeds that will allow the verifier to generate respectively the random permutation Σ and the $(m \times m)$ matrix Γ of rank weight w. Furthermore, we choose them such that $\ell_\Gamma + \ell_\Sigma < n$. This trick allowed us to reduce the cost of communication in our identification scheme. The properties of the repaired rank-based Véron's identification protocol are presented in the following Table 3.

Table 3. Properties of the repaired rank-based Véron identification scheme.

Size of the matrix in bits	$m \times k \times n$
Size of the public identification	$mn + \log_2(w)$
Size of the secret key	$mk + mn$
Total number of bits exchanged	$\delta(3h + 2 + \frac{2}{3}(\ell_\Gamma + \ell_\Sigma + m(k+n)))$

Since $\ell_\Gamma + \ell_\Sigma < n$ the number of bits exchanged in our scheme is lower than the scheme proposed by Bellini et al. (Table 1 and Table 3). Thus, in addition to being zero-knowledge, our identification scheme has a lower communication cost.

5.1 Security and Parameters

The zero-knowledge proof in this protocol is based on the RSD problem. We have to select parameters, especially w, for the Gilbert-Varshamov bound to avoid possible small rank attacks. We need to choose m, n, k, and w satisfying the following conditions:

— if the algebraic attack in [25] is applicable in the more generic scenario of $k < \lceil \frac{(k+1)(w+1)-(n+1)}{w} \rceil$, then we have $\log_2(w^3 k^3 q^{\lceil \frac{(k+1)(w+1)-(n+1)}{w} \rceil}) \geq \ell$ where ℓ is the security level.

- for the best known generic combinatorial attack [2], we have $\log_2((n - k)^3 m^3 q^{w\lceil \frac{(k+1)m}{n} \rceil - m}) \geq l$.

For the case of parameters that are secure even in the post-quantum setting, we will simply square-root the exponential term of the formula of each attack. We also need to choose the number of rounds δ to decrease the impersonation probability. In the Véron protocol the impersonation probability of one single round is $\frac{2}{3}$. To compute the number of round δ, we need to set $\delta = \log_2(1/2^\ell)$. We propose 2 sets of parameters as in Table 2, respectively for 80 and 128-bit security levels with the repaired identification scheme.

6 Signature Scheme

Using the Fiat-Shamir transformation [21], we can implement a signature scheme from our rank-based Véron identification scheme. We describe the signature process below.

6.1 Signing Procedure

In the first step, we compute a commitment cmt as:

$$\text{cmt} = (c_{01}, c_{02}, c_{03}) \| (c_{11}, c_{12}, c_{13}) \| \cdots \| (c_{\delta-1,1}, c_{\delta-1,2}, c_{\delta-1,3}) \quad (10)$$

In the second step, we compute the challenge ch = hash(cmt $\|$ msg), where msg is the message (typically the content of some file). Every two bits of ch give a partial challenge, where the bit pattern 11 is mapped to $b \in \{0, 1, 2\}$ cyclically.

Finally, we compute for each partial challenge b the response rsp_i ($0 \le i \le \delta$). Denote all responses by $\text{rsp} = (\text{rsp}_0 \parallel \text{rsp}_1 \parallel \cdots \parallel \text{rsp}_{\delta-1})$ and the final signature is $(\text{cmt} \parallel \text{rsp})$.

Prover	Verifier
sk, pk $= (x,e),(y,G,w)$	pk

$u \leftarrow\!\!\$\ \mathbb{F}_{q^m}^k,\ \Sigma \leftarrow\!\!\$\ S_n,\ \Gamma \leftarrow\!\!\$\ \mathbb{F}_q^{m \times m}$

$c_1 \leftarrow \textbf{hash}(\Gamma \parallel \Sigma)$

$c_2 \leftarrow \textbf{hash}(\Pi_{\Gamma,\Sigma}(u+x) \cdot G)$

$c_3 \leftarrow \textbf{hash}(\Pi_{\Gamma,\Sigma}(u \cdot G + y))$ $\qquad \xrightarrow{\ c_1, c_2, c_3\ }$

$\qquad\qquad\qquad\qquad\qquad \xleftarrow{\quad b \quad} \qquad b \leftarrow\!\!\$\ \{0,1,2\}$

if $b = 0$

$\quad \text{rsp}_1 \leftarrow \Gamma \parallel \ell_\Sigma,\ \text{rsp}_2 \leftarrow u + x$ $\xrightarrow{\ \text{rsp}_1,\ \text{rsp}_2\ }$ **if** $c_1 = \textbf{hash}(\text{rsp}_1)$ and

$\qquad\qquad\qquad\qquad\qquad\qquad\qquad\qquad\qquad c_2 = \textbf{hash}(\Pi_{\text{rsp}_1}(\text{rsp}_2 \cdot G))$

$\qquad\qquad\qquad\qquad\qquad\qquad\qquad\qquad\qquad$ **return true**

if $b = 1$

$\quad \text{rsp}_1 \leftarrow \Pi_{\Gamma,\Sigma}((u+x) \cdot G),$ $\xrightarrow{\ \text{rsp}_1,\ \text{rsp}_2\ }$ **if** $c_2 = \textbf{hash}(\text{rsp}_1)$ and

$\quad \text{rsp}_2 \leftarrow \Pi_{\Gamma,\Sigma}(e)$ $\qquad\qquad\qquad\qquad\qquad c_3 = \textbf{hash}(\text{rsp}_1 + \text{rsp}_2)$

$\qquad\qquad\qquad\qquad\qquad\qquad\qquad\qquad\qquad$ and $\textbf{r}(\text{rsp}_2) = w$

$\qquad\qquad\qquad\qquad\qquad\qquad\qquad\qquad\qquad$ **return true**

if $b = 2$

$\quad \text{rsp}_1 \leftarrow \Gamma \parallel \ell_\Sigma,\ \text{rsp}_2 \leftarrow u$ $\xrightarrow{\ \text{rsp}_1,\ \text{rsp}_2\ }$ **if** $c_1 = \textbf{hash}(\text{rsp}_1)$ and

$\qquad\qquad\qquad\qquad\qquad\qquad\qquad\qquad\qquad c_3 = \textbf{hash}(\Pi_{\text{rsp}_1}(\text{rsp}_2 \cdot G + y))$

$\qquad\qquad\qquad\qquad\qquad\qquad\qquad\qquad\qquad$ **return true**

Fig. 2. The repaired rank-based Véron's identification protocol

6.2 Verification Procedure

Once the signature is received, the verifier extracts cmt and computes ch $=$ $\textbf{hash}(\text{cmt} \parallel \text{msg})$. He uses the individual bytes of ch to obtain δ and challenges $b \in \{0,1,2\}$. Using b, he extracts the corresponding response contained in rsp and calculates the commitment c_{ij}, where $j = b$ and i denotes the current round. Finally, the verifier computes $\textbf{hash}(c_{ij})$ of cmt and compares this value with the c_{ij} contained in the triplet (c_{i1}, c_{i2}, c_{i3}). So we identify here the value $\textbf{hash}(c_{ij})$ and c_{ij}. If the values of c_{ij} match for all rounds, the signature is valid.

Our signature scheme in rank metric has the following keys and signature size:

- $|\textbf{sk}| = |x| + |e| = mk + nk$,
- $|\textbf{pk}| = |y| + |G| + |w| = mn + mkk + \log_2(w)$ (we use the systematic form of G),
- The average size of the signature is $|\textbf{sgn}| = |\text{cmt}| + |\text{rśp}| = \delta(3h + \frac{1}{3}(2m(k + n) + 2\ell_\Sigma + \alpha) + m^2)$.

6.3   Signature Comparison

In the Table 4, we compare our signature scheme for 128-bit security level with the best current post-quantum signature schemes. Schemes such as CRYSTALS-Dilithium, FALCON, and SPHINCS+ can be considered the best digital signatures and meet the NIST requirements. Therefore, future digital signatures must be significantly better than these winners of the standardization process in the relevant applications and/or guarantee substantial additional security properties. We also present alternative candidates for digital signatures such as Picnic [16] and GeMSS [13]. Picnic is a digital signature algorithm designed to provide security against quantum computer attacks. It uses only symmetric key primitives and is an instantiation of the MPC-in-the-head paradigm [28]. GeMSS is a multivariate-based signature. The public key for GeMSS is a multivariate quadratic system of equations over $\mathbb{F}_2$ and is built from the Hidden Field Equations (HFE) cryptosystem. In addition, we present results provided for the rank-based CVE identification [6], the first rank-based hash-and-sign signature scheme Wave [19], and Durandal [1], a variant of the Schnorr-Lyubashevsky approach for designing a rank-based cryptographic signature. We used 48-bit long seeds and a 256-bit hash function.

Table 4. Comparison of public keys and signature bit sizes of our scheme with the most popular code-based signature schemes. For numerical values, we have used the formulas in Sect. 6.2 with the same parameters in [6].

Scheme	Scheme parameters	|sgn|	|pk|
CRYSTALS-Dilithium	(mod, d, η, δ)	2 420	1 312
FALCON-512	(8380417,13,2,78) (mod, n, δ)	666	897
SPHINCS+	(12289,512,165.736) $(n, h, d, log(t), k, w)$	17 088	64
GeMSS	(16,66,22,6,33,16) $(\lambda, D, n, \Delta, v, \text{nb-ite})$	32.25	360 640,512
Picnic	128,513,174,12,12,4) (N, M, δ)	12 288	64
Wave	(64,343,27) (n, k, w, k_U, k_V)	8 326	7 840 000
Durandal	(5172,3908,4980,2299,1609) $(q, n, m, k, w, l, l', d, r, \lambda)$	40 150	148 851
CVE-128	(2,226,263,113,56,4,1,7,7,14) $(q, n, m, k, w, \delta, h)$	27 389 952	310 084
Our scheme-128	(2,64,80,30,9,128,256) $(q, n, m, k, w, \delta, h)$ (2,64,80,30,9,219,256)	2 679 392	77 124

From the Table 4, we can see that our signature scheme aligns with most code-based identification schemes. Compared to other code-based signature systems, we have a slightly larger but acceptable signature size of 2.7 million bits. But we have the smallest public key size of 77 thousand bits, which allows us to have a fast verification time. For other digital signatures that are considered the best at the moment, our key size is also competitive. For example, we are better than GeMSS with 360 thousand bits of public key size which was considered a credible alternative to the NIST standardization process for digital signature. As far as security is concerned, our signature scheme is beyond the reach of existing attacks on code-based signatures.

7   Conclusion

In this paper, we first presented a full cryptanalysis of the scheme presented in [6]. This attack takes advantage of the structure of hiding the secret e by a simple permutation in $\mathbb{F}_{q^m}$. This weakness in this scheme allowed us to recover the error support and thus break the scheme in polynomial time using the algorithm of Gaborit, Ruatta, and Schreck. Second, we proposed a new rank-based identification protocol. The masking of the e secret is achieved using a special permutation that avoids information leakage during the response phase of our identification scheme. Finally, we presented a signature scheme with low communication cost and a small public key size that allows us to perform fast verification. Our scheme is overall resilient against attacks on quantum computers.

References

1. Aragon, N., Blazy, O., Gaborit, P., Hauteville, A., Zémor, G.: Durandal: a rank metric based signature scheme. In: Ishai, Y., Rijmen, V. (eds.) EUROCRYPT 2019. LNCS, vol. 11478, pp. 728–758. Springer, Cham (2019). https://doi.org/10.1007/978-3-030-17659-4_25
2. Aragon, N., Gaborit, P., Hauteville, A., Tillich, J.P.: A new algorithm for solving the rank syndrome decoding problem. In: 2018 IEEE International Symposium on Information Theory (ISIT), pp. 2421–2425. IEEE (2018)
3. Baldi, M., et al.: A new path to code-based signatures via identification schemes with restricted errors. arXiv preprint arXiv:2008.06403 (2020)
4. Becker, A., Joux, A., May, A., Meurer, A.: Decoding random binary linear codes in $2^{n/20}$: how 1+1=0 improves information set decoding. In: Pointcheval, D., Johansson, T. (eds.) EUROCRYPT 2012. LNCS, vol. 7237, pp. 520–536. Springer, Heidelberg (2012). https://doi.org/10.1007/978-3-642-29011-4_31
5. Bellini, E., Caullery, F., Gaborit, P., Manzano, M., Mateu, V.: Improved veron identification and signature schemes in the rank metric. In: IEEE International Symposium on Information Theory, ISIT 2019, Paris, France, 7–12 July 2019, pp. 1872–1876. IEEE (2019). https://doi.org/10.1109/ISIT.2019.8849585
6. Bellini, E., Caullery, F., Hasikos, A., Manzano, M., Mateu, V.: Code-based signature schemes from identification protocols in the rank metric. In: Camenisch, J., Papadimitratos, P. (eds.) CANS 2018. LNCS, vol. 11124, pp. 277–298. Springer, Cham (2018). https://doi.org/10.1007/978-3-030-00434-7_14

7. Bellini, E., Gaborit, P., Hasikos, A., Mateu, V.: Enhancing code based zero-knowledge proofs using rank metric. IACR Cryptol. ePrint Arch. **2020**, 1472 (2020), https://eprint.iacr.org/2020/1472

8. Berlekamp, E., McEliece, R., Van Tilborg, H.: On the inherent intractability of certain coding problems (corresp.). IEEE Trans. Inf. Theor. **24**(3), 384–386 (1978)

9. Bernstein, D.J.: Grover vs. McEliece. In: Sendrier, N. (ed.) PQCrypto 2010. LNCS, vol. 6061, pp. 73–80. Springer, Heidelberg (2010). https://doi.org/10.1007/978-3-642-12929-2_6

10. Bernstein, D.J., Hülsing, A., Kölbl, S., Niederhagen, R., Rijneveld, J., Schwabe, P.: The sphincs+ signature framework. In: Proceedings of the 2019 ACM SIGSAC Conference on Computer and Communications Security, pp. 2129–2146 (2019)

11. Both, L., May, A.: Optimizing BJMM with nearest neighbors: full decoding in 22/21n and McEliece security. In: WCC Workshop on Coding and Cryptography (2017)

12. Both, L., May, A.: Decoding linear codes with high error rate and its impact for LPN security. In: Lange, T., Steinwandt, R. (eds.) PQCrypto 2018. LNCS, vol. 10786, pp. 25–46. Springer, Cham (2018). https://doi.org/10.1007/978-3-319-79063-3_2

13. Casanova, A., Faugere, J., Macario-Rat, G., Patarin, J., Perret, L., Ryckeghem, J.: Gemss. submission to the NIST post-quantum cryptography standardization project (2020)

14. Cayrel, P.-L., Véron, P., El Yousfi Alaoui, S.M.: A zero-knowledge identification scheme based on the q-ary syndrome decoding problem. In: Biryukov, A., Gong, G., Stinson, D.R. (eds.) SAC 2010. LNCS, vol. 6544, pp. 171–186. Springer, Heidelberg (2011). https://doi.org/10.1007/978-3-642-19574-7_12

15. Chabaud, F., Stern, J.: The cryptographic security of the syndrome decoding problem for rank distance codes. In: Kim, K., Matsumoto, T. (eds.) ASIACRYPT 1996. LNCS, vol. 1163, pp. 368–381. Springer, Heidelberg (1996). https://doi.org/10.1007/BFb0034862

16. Chase, M., et al.: The picnic signature scheme (2020)

17. Chen, K.: A new identification algorithm. In: Dawson, E., Golić, J. (eds.) CPA 1995. LNCS, vol. 1029, pp. 244–249. Springer, Heidelberg (1996). https://doi.org/10.1007/BFb0032363

18. Courtois, N.T., Finiasz, M., Sendrier, N.: How to achieve a McEliece-based digital signature scheme. In: Boyd, C. (ed.) ASIACRYPT 2001. LNCS, vol. 2248, pp. 157–174. Springer, Heidelberg (2001). https://doi.org/10.1007/3-540-45682-1_10

19. Debris-Alazard, T., Sendrier, N., Tillich, J.-P.: Wave: a new family of trapdoor one-way preimage sampleable functions based on codes. In: Galbraith, S.D., Moriai, S. (eds.) ASIACRYPT 2019. LNCS, vol. 11921, pp. 21–51. Springer, Cham (2019). https://doi.org/10.1007/978-3-030-34578-5_2

20. Dumer, I.: On minimum distance decoding of linear codes. In: Proceedings 5th Joint Soviet-Swedish International Workshop Information Theory, pp. 50–52 (1991)

21. Fiat, A., Shamir, A.: How to prove yourself: practical solutions to identification and signature problems. In: Odlyzko, A.M. (ed.) CRYPTO 1986. LNCS, vol. 263, pp. 186–194. Springer, Heidelberg (1987). https://doi.org/10.1007/3-540-47721-7_12

22. Finiasz, M., Sendrier, N.: Security bounds for the design of code-based cryptosystems. In: Matsui, M. (ed.) ASIACRYPT 2009. LNCS, vol. 5912, pp. 88–105. Springer, Heidelberg (2009). https://doi.org/10.1007/978-3-642-10366-7_6

23. Fouque, P.A., Hoffstein, J., Kirchner, P., Lyubashevsky, V., Pornin, T., Prest, T., Ricosset, T., Seiler, G., Whyte, W., Zhang, Z.: Falcon: Fast-fourier lattice-based compact signatures over NTRU. Submission NIST Post-Quantum Crypt. Stand.-Round **36**(5) (2020)
24. Gabidulin, E.M.: Theory of codes with maximum rank distance. Problemy Peredachi Informatsii **21**(1), 3–16 (1985)
25. Gaborit, P., Ruatta, O., Schrek, J.: On the complexity of the rank syndrome decoding problem. IEEE Trans. Inf. Theory **62**(2), 1006–1019 (2015)
26. Gaborit, P., Schrek, J., Zémor, G.: Full cryptanalysis of the Chen identification protocol. In: Yang, B.-Y. (ed.) PQCrypto 2011. LNCS, vol. 7071, pp. 35–50. Springer, Heidelberg (2011). https://doi.org/10.1007/978-3-642-25405-5_3
27. Harari, S.: A new authentication algorithm. In: Cohen, G., Wolfmann, J. (eds.) Coding Theory 1988. LNCS, vol. 388, pp. 91–105. Springer, Heidelberg (1989). https://doi.org/10.1007/BFb0019849
28. Ishai, Y., Kushilevitz, E., Ostrovsky, R., Sahai, A.: Zero-knowledge from secure multiparty computation. In: Proceedings of the Thirty-ninth Annual ACM Symposium on Theory of Computing, pp. 21–30 (2007)
29. Kachigar, G., Tillich, J.-P.: Quantum information set decoding algorithms. In: Lange, T., Takagi, T. (eds.) PQCrypto 2017. LNCS, vol. 10346, pp. 69–89. Springer, Cham (2017). https://doi.org/10.1007/978-3-319-59879-6_5
30. Lamport, L.: Constructing digital signatures from a one way function (1979)
31. Lau, T.S.C., Tan, C.H., Prabowo, T.F.: Key recovery attacks on some rank metric code-based signatures. In: Albrecht, M. (ed.) IMACC 2019. LNCS, vol. 11929, pp. 215–235. Springer, Cham (2019). https://doi.org/10.1007/978-3-030-35199-1_11
32. van Lint, J.H., Wilson, R.M.: A Course in Combinatorics. Cambridge University Press, New York (2001)
33. Loidreau, P.: Properties of codes in rank metric. arXiv preprint cs/0610057 (2006)
34. Lyubashevsky, V., et al.: Crystals-dilithium. Submission NIST Post-Quantum Crypt. Stand.-Round **3** (2020)
35. May, A., Ozerov, I.: On computing nearest neighbors with applications to decoding of binary linear codes. In: Oswald, E., Fischlin, M. (eds.) EUROCRYPT 2015. LNCS, vol. 9056, pp. 203–228. Springer, Heidelberg (2015). https://doi.org/10.1007/978-3-662-46800-5_9
36. McEliece, R.J.: A public-key cryptosystem based on algebraic. Coding Thv **4244**, 114–116 (1978)
37. Ourivski, A.V., Johansson, T.: New technique for decoding codes in the rank metric and its cryptography applications. Prob. Inf. Transm. **38**(3), 237–246 (2002)
38. Peters, C.: Information-set decoding for linear codes over $\mathbf{F}$ q </Subscript>. In: Sendrier, N. (ed.) PQCrypto 2010. LNCS, vol. 6061, pp. 81–94. Springer, Heidelberg (2010). https://doi.org/10.1007/978-3-642-12929-2_7 </Subscript>. In: Sendrier, N. (ed.) PQCrypto 2010. LNCS, vol. 6061, pp. 81–94. Springer, Heidelberg (2010). https://doi.org/10.1007/978-3-642-12929-2_7
39. Prange, E.: The use of information sets in decoding cyclic codes. IRE Trans. Inf. Theory **8**(5), 5–9 (1962)
40. Shor, P.W.: Algorithms for quantum computation: discrete logarithms and factoring. In: Proceedings 35th Annual Symposium on Foundations of Computer Science, pp. 124–134. IEEE (1994)

41. Stern, J.: A method for finding codewords of small weight. In: Cohen, G., Wolfmann, J. (eds.) Coding Theory 1988. LNCS, vol. 388, pp. 106–113. Springer, Heidelberg (1989). https://doi.org/10.1007/BFb0019850
42. Stern, J.: A new identification scheme based on syndrome decoding. In: Stinson, D.R. (ed.) CRYPTO 1993. LNCS, vol. 773, pp. 13–21. Springer, Heidelberg (1994). https://doi.org/10.1007/3-540-48329-2_2
43. Véron, P.: Improved identification schemes based on error-correcting codes. Appl. Algebra Eng. Commun. Comput. 8(1), 57–69 (1997)

An Embedded AI-Based Smart Intrusion Detection System for Edge-to-Cloud Systems

Ritu-Ranjan Shrivastwa[(⊠)] [iD], Zakaria Bouakka, Thomas Perianin,
Fabrice Dislaire, Tristan Gaudron, Youssef Souissi, Khaled Karray,
and Sylvain Guilley [iD]

Secure-IC S.A.S., 15 Rue Claude Chappe Bât. B, 35510 Cesson-Sévigné, France
{ritu-ranjan.shrivastwa,zakaria.bouakka,thomas.perianin,fabrice.dislaire,
tristan.gaudron,youssef.souissi,khaled.karray,
sylvain.guilley}@secure-ic.com
https://www.secure-ic.com/

Abstract. This article proposes a general purpose IoT framework usually applicable to all Edge-to-Cloud applications and provides an evaluation study on a use-case involving automotive V2X architecture, tested and verified on a toy smart-car in an emulated smart-car environment. The architecture in study is finely tuned to mimic actual scenarios and therefore the sensors available on the toy car encompasses almost all the sensors that assist a regular ADAS in smart cars of today. The cloud connectivity is maintained through the CoAP protocol which is a standard IoT connectivity protocol. Finally, the security solution proposed is that of a smart Intrusion Detection System (IDS) that is built using Machine Learning (ML) technique and is deployed on the edge. The edge IDS is capable of performing anomaly detection and reporting both detection results as well as sensor collected big data to the cloud. On the cloud side the server stores and maintains the collected data for further retraining of ML models for edge anomaly detection which is differentiated into two categories viz. sensor anomaly detection model and network anomaly detection model. To demonstrate Software update Over The Air (SW-OTA) the cloud in the evaluation setup implements a ML model upgrade capability from the cloud to the connected edge. This implementation and evaluation provides a Proof-of-Concept of the choice of ML as IDS candidate and the framework in general to be applicable to various other IoT scenarios such as Healthcare, Smart-home, Smart-city, Harbour and Industrial environments, and so on, and paves way for future optimization studies.

Keywords: Edge computing · Artificial intelligence · Cybersecurity services · Embedded security · Anomaly detection · Intrusion detection systems · V2X · Internet of Things · Advanced Driver Assistance Systems) (ADAS)

A. Nitaj and K. Zkik (Eds.): I4CS 2022, CCIS 1747, pp. 20–39, 2022.
https://doi.org/10.1007/978-3-031-23201-5_2

1   Introduction

The connected device market is getting flooded as technology becomes more scalable and computing resources at the device level increased. Thus, the IoT is no longer a fancy concept and has become the need to solve the real-time crisis as researchers observe possibilities to optimize livelihood in every sector of human civilization through a properly connected device infrastructure. This in turn is boosting the growth of standards and protocols to unify the development process which also, not so surprisingly, is opening new attack surfaces. Autonomous cars are running along-side manual cars and Artificial Intelligence is diagnosing medical symptoms in patients. The applications of sensing and actuation and end nodes of a IoT network are in fact pushing the Data Scientists to properly handle the generated Big Data streams and utilize it to improve the services for the end customers. Implementing sophisticated features implies that the security needs to be inherently robust to handle such complex system and therefore, prevent from compromising the whole system since, depending upon the use-case, there might be a safety risk involved. To prevent the exploitation of the smart solutions by adversaries on the edge side which is exposed to threat actors, it is important to have a smart solution that is able to track minute differences in operational environment and alert the mother system at the edge or cloud level.

The motivation behind this work is to propose a smart Intrusion Detection System (IDS) in a connected edge-to-cloud system that is capable of sensing from every sensory node available on board and aggregate the results of anomaly detection from each and report back to the cloud. This is achieved by mimicking the architecture of a smart car (V2X) ecosystem (where the car is connected to the cloud and its locomotion greatly depends on its on-board sensors) through a toy smart car and emulated environment with dedicated threats with a nearly full coverage on all sensing equipment on the toy smart car.

The idea is to emulate threats at both sensor and network level (all possible attacks to disrupt the functionality of the smart car) and develop a system capable enough to observe these differences in a real-time scenario. The experimental setup consists of a toy smart car with on-board sensor array connected to the internal IDS which is composed of two separate Machine Learning (ML) cores, one for detecting anomalies through the sensor data and one for detecting anomalies through the network data (packets). The toy smart car is connected to a cloud server through popular IoT connectivity protocol CoAP and transmits detection signal back to the cloud along with the collected data from the sensor and network. Through careful and lengthy evaluation of a multitude of scenarios and through a rigorous experimentation process, we find that the proposed IDS is suitable to a wide variety of input data and therefore can be universally applied to any IoT use-case.

The rest of the paper is organized as follows: the Sect. 2 provides a generic background of topics linked with the proposed work by running through the problem statement and navigating through the solution while talking about various aspects of the system. It also provides some common standards that are (being) developed to streamline IoT product development. Next, the Sect. 3 provides the details about the proposed method with details about the evaluation concept, experimental setup, and results. It also talks about the implications of the same in the real world. Finally, the Sect. 4 presents other important topics that are extremely relevant, and acclaimed by technology providers, to the edge-to-cloud ecosystem. Eventually, Sect. 5 concludes the paper.

2   General Background

2.1   Edge-to-Cloud

Today's devices are clearly becoming smarter by having more and more interactions with the outside world. Such interaction is offering much more capabilities and obviously opening new ways for new applications targeting most of technology ecosystems such as connected vehicles, Industry 4.0, smart cities, healthcare, smart agriculture, smart homes, etc. In the literature, those smart devices are often called edge devices if they have the capability to ensure back-and-forth connectivity with other devices or with a central system that we call Cloud server in the sequel. The edge device is basically composed of a processing unit that can be an MCU with low resources or an MPU with more power and computing resources. edge devices themselves can be used as bridges between a server and Internet of Things objects (IoT). Typically, we can define an edge-to-Cloud system as a technology composed of three main actors as follows:

- **Actor 1:** the edge device that comes with a connectivity module, alongside a host CPU for the software, and a hardware layer.
- **Actor 2:** the sever side is a machine with much more power and computing capabilities. It is a central element that talks with a fleet of edge devices. The server shall come with application services to manage and monitor the connected devices.
- **Actor 3:** the user interacting with the server to send requests to edge devices and monitor the fleet of edge devices. Users could have different privileges and roles with regards to the server.

An illustration of such system is depicted in Fig. 1.

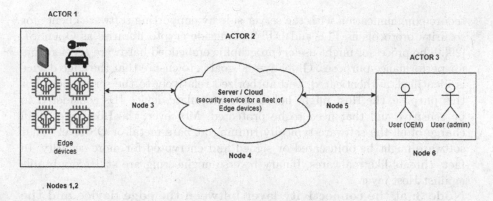

Fig. 1. Edge-to-cloud main nodes and actors.

Very often, any similar technology faces two basic challenges, namely security and performance. Safety is a third challenge that shall be considered for related technologies as automotive and avionics. In the sequel we focus only on security. In fact, security is the way how data is protected. The data is by default sensitive and can be everywhere, at rest or in-transit. Based on the Fig. 1, we can distinguish 6 nodes where end-to-end security shall be considered in edge-to-Cloud context as follows:

– **Node 1: at the hardware layer of the edge device.** The security here is generally managed by a technology dependent secure layer as a Trusted Execution Environment (TEE), Trusted Platform Module (TPM), or a dedicated Secure Element (SE), as described here [24]. Such layer ensures a strong security level as per data isolation, secure storage of secrets, etc. A TEE consists in separating the same Host processor into two spaces: normal space and secure space. All security operations shall run within the secure space by ensuring an isolation with the normal space. However, such security mechanism is less secure than a dedicated hardware as TPM or SE. In fact, within a TEE, the shared components as internal Host processor memories might leak sensitive data. The TPM is theoretically more secure than TEE as it comes with a separated hardware chip. However, the leakage might come from the link between the Host processor and the TPM. In fact, the data in transit might be probed and stolen if not encrypted. Finally, an integrated secure element shall be the most secure as it is embedded in the same SoC as Host processor. That said, physical attacks such as Side-channel attacks (SCA) [17] or Fault injection attacks (FIA) [5] are the first enemy against the hardware layer. Fortunately, countermeasures like data hiding exist.
– **Node 2: at the CPU Host layer of the edge device.** The security of data shall be considered by the Host processor that would implement a software bridge handling a secure channel with the server side. The Host processor shall be able to use cryptographic software engines if security hardware components are not available. For this purpose, the processor shall manage the

secure communication with the server side by supporting software clients for security protocols as TLS and DTLS alongside crypto libraries as OpenSSL [29]. The processor might use cryptographic embedded hardware accelerators for performance purposes. Globally, the goal is to ensure that the edge device is identified, authenticated, and authorized relatively to the server side. For this purpose, the Host might hold and manipulate device IDs considered to be sensitive and that need to be protected. Moreover, the Host layer is in charge of all the software typically running at bare metal or OS level. That software might be obfuscated or signed and encrypted for more security. In fact, threats like malwares, binary reverse engineering are still redoubtable against Host layer.

- **Node 3: at the connectivity layer between the edge device and the server.** The connectivity layer is all about network stack ranging from the physical channel to applicative protocols. Edge devices are basically communicating over IP-based channels as Ethernet, WiFi, Cellular (4G, 5G, 6G, etc.), etc. Some RF protocols use an encapsulation technique to allow IP-based communication. The security shall consider all the layers of the network. The OSI model for instance suggests securing the lowest layers with MACSec (for data link) or IPSec (for transport). Then application protocols are proposed as TLS and DTLS. Higher applicative frameworks for connectivity like LwM2M, MQTTS come with a set of schemes to securely manage a device. As a matter of fact, LwM2M is based on CoAP and DTLS protocols to initiate a communication with an edge device.
- **Node 4: at the server core layer including its data storage components.** The server is the central element in the system. It manages the input and output data from edge devices. Security is a big matter and should at least be ensured for the data at rest like edge devices' logs and users' credentials, often stored in databases; data in transit like direct requests from users to edge devices; or also the server components and interactions between those components themselves. In fact, the server is the most impacted node as it is exposed to internet. In other words, it is the target of a tremendous number of cyberattacks. As a matter of fact, a long list of cyberattacks is regularly updated by the OWASP web pentesting framework group. Hence, security shall be thoroughly checked from the server infrastructure level to applicative micro-services. The literature has recently proposed a new approach with several security requirements, called "zero-trust", that aims at maximizing the security at cloud server node.
- **Node 5: at the connectivity layer between the server and the user machine.** Same as for node 3, the connectivity here is more about the relationship between the user and the server. The security of this node is crucial as it deals with user credentials and devices registration initial inputs alongside secret data as keys and certificates. Thankfully, a known approach called IAM that stands for Identity Access Management, comes with a set of tools, protocols, and frameworks to securely authenticate, and authorize users to access the server. We cite 0Auth2 [14] for instance. In addition to that, security could be reinforced by a double authentication technique as it

is proposed by FIDO2. Moreover, the security could be maximal by combining such software-based solutions with hardware tokens. The attack surface is about letting data to be transferred as plaintext without any mutual authentication or privilege mechanism. The attacks are numerous like data sniffing, probing, fuzzing, man-in-the-middle, etc.

- **Node 6: at the user machine level.** This node regards the user machine that interacts with the server side. Most commonly known attacks are performed on software web browsers and interfaces. Technically, this represents the front-side of the server solution that can be a web interface, a web application, a command line interface, an exposed API, etc. The security scope is about all the known attacks as SQL injections against databases, cross-site scripting attacks (XSS), traversal directory attacks, etc.

2.2 AI and Machine Learning for Anomaly and Intrusion Detection

Artificial Intelligence (AI) and particularly the Machine Learning (ML) subfield provide powerful prediction algorithms that constitute state-of-the-art techniques in several research areas: image processing, natural language processing, medical diagnosis, etc. Naturally, those methods are also drawing increasing interest in the cybersecurity landscape. Indeed, the advanced modelling capabilities of ML algorithms allow to leverage on large quantities of available data and knowledge to improve security systems in various fields of application. ML approaches are perfectly suited for attack or failure detection applications as they allow creating a model of the normal predictable behavior of a system [25]. After this profiling phase, it becomes possible to detect significant deviations from the model. A typical example of application are intrusion detection systems which analyse a network traffic to detect, block and report malicious packets. A "traditional" IDS uses a database of known malicious signatures that compares with the incoming packets to detect attacks. This approach presents a significant drawback: it detects attacks based on known threats and is unable to handle new attacks. On the other hand, it is possible to use ML algorithms to create a model of the normal behaviour of a network and to detect abnormal activities based on the observed deviations from the base profile. This approach has the advantage of detecting unknown or zero-day attacks.

The same idea can be applied to sensor data analysis. Standard deployment of fleet of sensors requires calibration, and threshold-based analysis is necessary to process sensor values, which often leads to false positives. AI-based sensor aggregation and analysis enable detection of fault injection attacks, anomalies and failures, and advanced diagnosis [11], while reducing the number of false alerts. To build such a system, a test chip is characterized in controlled environment, in order to generate sample data and train a detection model to be deployed on the final chip. Then, in operation, the model classifies new data, provide useful information (attack? anomaly? failure? type of attack?) and report to upper layers. Based on desired security policy or user feedback, the detection sensibility can also be adapted after deployment.

It is worth mentioning that AI techniques can also be used as tools to conduct attacks or assist security evaluations. For example, in the field of side-channel analysis, ML-based methods are employed to process measurements obtained during the execution of a security target to extract secret values such as private keys [21]. However, Machine Learning systems can also be the target of attacks, Typically, fault injections attacks can be used to fault the computation of a neural network and to bypass a security verification. More recently, a whole new class of attacks, called adversarial attacks [13], have been designed to fool ML algorithms by crafting malicious inputs which can go through neural network-based detection.

2.3   Connectivity

Over the past years, the rise of IoT market highlighted the need for efficient communication layers with small footprint, allowing low end devices like sensors or cameras to ensure low power consumption, low network bandwidth and a long living time if powered by a battery.

In the edge-to-cloud context, some protocols emerged and were standardized by the industry for machine to machine (M2M) communication. We can mention the most commonly used ones:

- Message Queue Telemetry Transport (MQTT) [28], based on the publish-subscribe methodology allowing one-to-many communication through brokers.
- Constrained Application Protocol (CoAP) [27], a client-server protocol offering a RESTful interface allowing a client node to directly command another node.

Both protocols are IP-based and come with activable security features: MQTTS using TLS for MQTT, and DTLS or IPSec for CoAP, ensuring transport encryption and mutual authentication.

More recently, higher level protocols including an application layer have been presented as standards. OMA Lightweight M2M (LwM2M) [4] is a protocol for device management and service enablement, defining the application layer communication protocol between a server and a client, which is the IoT device. In the same way, the Matter protocol (previously known as Project CHIP) [2] for home automation connectivity is being standardized. It promises interoperability among smart home devices from different vendors and IoT platforms.

2.4   Security Standards and Frameworks

The aforementioned edge-to-cloud type IoT systems involve massive data transfer through the network that includes sensitive information, unauthorized access to which might jeopardize the whole system leading to security and even safety related hazards. Therefore, such systems are equipped with state-of-the-art cyber-security mechanisms to deal with security threats and intrusions. To ensure a secure development and assure the consumer of the degree of competence and robustness of the systems in terms of security features, it is essential to go through the certification process of such products. Any edge-to-cloud system might fall under a typical IoT framework and therefore it becomes quintessential to secure the system based on standard practices. The widely acclaimed certification schemes that would help reach such standards of security are listed below:

1. **Common Criteria (CC)** - The [7] (ISO/IEC 15408) provides seven assurance levels based on which any general purpose product can be certified. The framework is based on the IT product security but the presence of protection profiles makes it more suited for different market verticals. Certification with CC is gaining momentum for IoT products as more and more companies enter to compete with this product line, since IoT has already reached to our homes.
2. **SESIP** [12] is a platform-level certification scheme for IoTs, promoted by the Global Platform association. It is meant to be similar in the rigor to the CC albeit with a more simple applicability.
3. **FIPS 140-3** - The FIPS 140-3 [19] (ISO/IEC 19790) from the NIST (USA) is an upgrade over the extremely popular FIPS 140-2 standard. It provides a technical baseline for security products and can be easily framed around IoT ecosystem. With four distinct levels of security, the Cryptographic Module Verification Program (CMVP) ensures that the security of the product is optimized as per the security scope.
4. **ENISA Cloud certification scheme** ENISA [9] is a popular and respected European agency for cybersecurity that provides useful standards from time to time. In 2020, it provided a draft certification scheme for cloud based applications targeting the IoT edge-to-cloud products.
5. **Eurosmart IoT certification scheme** This standard [10] based on the European Cybersecurity Act, provides a targeted framework for IoT products with three different levels of security such as basic, substantial, and high.
6. **PSA Certified** Similar to the CC, the PSA Certified [22] provides third-party lab evaluation for security assurance for IoT product vendors and manufacturers with three distinct assurance levels.

3 Monitoring Cyber Use-Case

This section describes our proposed embedded IDS architecture and implementation, designed to be deployed on fleets of devices in the context of IoT monitoring.

3.1 Typical Architecture

The proposed IDS is comprised of multiple anomaly detection cores, each one being in charge of processing a different type of inputs. The IDS can be deployed with a variable number of detection cores, depending on the target device. The architecture described in this paper contains two cores: for WLAN connectivity and for sensors. Additional cores can be plugged, for CAN intrusion detection for instance. Each core has access to a local storage where a detection model is stored. The global architecture is summarized in Fig. 2 for an automotive use-case which we chose for the evaluation in our work.

A COAP server is used for bi-directional communication with the cloud server side: on one hand, for sending notifications to the cloud and on the other hand, for configuring the edge IDS from the cloud server. The cloud is equipped with tools for monitoring real-time data from the connected device and displays anomaly notification.

The edge, along with the telemetry of core anomaly detectors, also uploads the aggregated sensor data. This data is collected in the cloud in a desired format which is later used for offline-training to further tune the Machine Learning core. Finally, the cloud has the capability, through the CoAP channel, to push a new ML model with newly trained/tuned parameters based on more collected data on the edge, and update the Intrusion Detection System. This is a typical Software update Over The Air (SW-OTA).

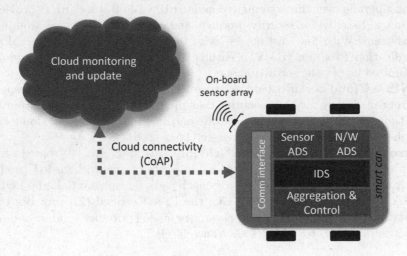

Fig. 2. Typical edge-to-cloud architecture.

3.2 Security Threats and Attack Surface

The attack surface of an edge device varies from case to case, depending on its connectivity features (WiFi, Bluetooth, etc), its hardware and software architectures (OS, bare metal, microcontroller or pure hardware) but in most cases, we can identify the following threats:

– Fault Injection Attacks (FIA)
  This class of attack consists in actively stressing a system in order to compromise its security. In short, when perturbing a security system, an attacker can induce faults during a computation or generate bit-flips in memory cells.

Those effects can then be exploited for sensitive variable recovery, for example with differential fault analysis (DFA) [8] or to skip specific instructions in order to bypass a security mechanism. There are several physical channels that can be used to generate the perturbation: power glitching, clock glitching, by temperature, electromagnetic injection, laser injection, etc., as well as software or hybrid methods [23].

Fault tolerant systems can be designed at the cost of performance: those systems use redundancy as countermeasure for fault injection attacks, in various ways: statically (e.g. second order statements, step counters), or dynamically (e.g. checksums, control-flow graph redundancy). Active defense against fault injection consists of analysing sensors values to detect attacks at runtime: this approach, enhanced with machine learning, is one of the focus of the IDS presented in this paper.

– Connectivity related cyberattacks
These attacks target communication interfaces of the devices. Multiple attacks can be realized, with various objectives. Some examples are detailed here.

Denial of Service (DoS) attacks aim at flooding a service with traffic in order to prevent the device to operate correctly, for example by occupying all the available bandwidth, consuming all the device resources, making the system crash or preventing legitimate traffic to reach its destination.

Address Resolution Protocol (ARP) spoofing is a different type of attack where the attacker aims at impersonating a valid host device, causing the target device to send any traffic directed at the true host to the attacker instead. The attacker can then listen to the packets, discard them, or falsify them before sending them to the true host, achieving a Man-in-the-Middle (MiTM) position. ARP is a protocol used in Ethernet and WiFi to resolve a MAC address given an IP address. Devices can broadcast ARP requests to a network when they need the MAC address associated to a certain IP (in this case, the IP of the host). Anyone connected to the network can reply with an ARP response. Since ARP does not support any authentication mechanism, an attacker can send fake ARP responses containing its own MAC address, causing the target to send packets to the attacker instead of the host. However, during such an attack, the attacker generates unusual activity on the network which can be detected by an intrusion detection system.

Lastly, **port scanning** consists in scanning each port in a network in order to discover which ports are open and whether they give access to vulnerable applications. While actually not an attack, this malicious behaviour can be detected by an intrusion detection system.

The IDS framework presented in this paper is designed to handle connectivity related cyberattacks with a focus on the TCP/IP network interface.

– Side Channel Attacks (SCA)
Side Channel Attacks are a type of passive attacks where the attacker "listens" to a system during a sensitive computation, through a physical channel like the power consumption or EM emanations, in order to discover the sensitive

information being processed. This often implies using physical equipment to generate measurements and employing statistical tools to process those traces and extract the secret values. Some side-channel attacks can be conducted entirely by software, with no physical access to the device [1].

Side-channel attacks, because they passive, are not in the scope of the detection framework presented in this paper. However, runtime detection of cache-based side channel attacks is an area of research as the malicious processes performing those attacks have observable side effects on hardware performance counters, which can be characterized as abnormal behavior. In future works, it could be considered to extend the scope of the proposed IDS to specific types of side channel attacks.

– Application level attacks
  On rich edge devices containing an operating system and applications, attacks can target directly vulnerabilities present in software applications, such as stack buffer overflows. This part of the attack surface is not covered by this paper. In many cases, those attacks can be prevented by source code analysis or dynamic testing.

3.3 On-Board Intrusion Detection

The main challenge on the edge is to aggregate all the sensor information from various channels and detect abnormalities or falsified perturbation and detect a difference (glitch) using ML, pertaining to the whole system. In this work we try to classify a normal scenario (un-perturbed case) and an anomalous scenario while the smart car is in motion. In order to ensure good training, the data is significant. Therefore, separate sessions were run to collect different types of data. As mentioned earlier, two anomaly detectors are embedded within the edge viz. sensor anomaly detector and network anomaly detector. The sensors data recorded is from a variety of sensors including:

1. **External:** Ultrasonic ranger, Camera, LDR sensor, IR sensors (for lines-tracing in the test area), Gyroscope, Accelerometer, Magnetometer, Barometer, Temperature and Humidity Sensor;
2. **Internal:** CPU temperature, clock, voltage, memory split, throttle status.

Apart from the sensors, the Network packet data is also monitored for anomalous activity. In order to collect precise data without any phase difference, an additional on-board system called the data aggregation unit is installed to collect inputs from all sensors and stack them together balancing the phase. Once the data is collected, the training for the sensor and network anomaly detectors is carried out. The training process is completed as shown in the Fig. 3.

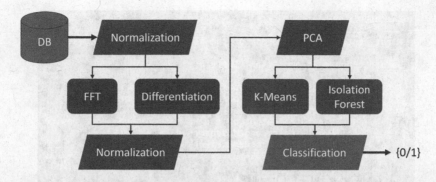

Fig. 3. Anomaly detection ML core training and model generation flow diagram.

ATTACK IMPLEMENTED	Non-contact to ground (accidental lift-off)	Collision	Humidity	Ultrasonic sensors spoofing	TCP DoS	Nmap	ARP poisoning
IDS DETECTION	Very good	Very good	Very good	Not at all	Very good	Very good	Poor
DETAILED RESULT (PRECISION, RECALL)	Ø	Ø	Ø	Ø	(71%, 83%)	(52%, 92%)	Ø
SENSORS INVOLVED (A PRIORI)	pressure sensor, thermometer, humidity sensor, photoresistors, accelerometer, gyroscope, magnetometer, ultrasonic sensors	pressure, temperature, humidity, photoresistors, accelerometers, gyroscopes, magnetometers, ultrasonic sensors	humidity sensor	ultrasonic sensors	network	network	network

Fig. 4. Results table.

Results. The results obtained from testing the robot smart car with different attacks involving both sensors as well as network, are highlighted below in the Fig. 4.

The on-board IDS could easily detect both the sensor anomalous activity as well as the network anomalous packet activity. Thus, securing the Proof-of-Concept (PoC) of the designated motivation of having a generic framework of Intrusion Detection System for IoT systems (in our case a **V2X** scenario) by running smart filtration of sensor and network activity (surfaces prone to threats from different adversarial actors) including both human-error (accidents, improper operation, etc.) as well as induced faults, to detect and classify them against normal operation. Additionally, it connects to the cloud for sending both real-time (with only latency due to connectivity) anomaly detection status as well as collected sensor data which is used to re-train existing anomaly detection ML models or new models on the cloud and push new ML core models to the edge. The capabilities of the cloud services available for our use-case are shown in Fig. 5.

```
* The user's guide:

* First, enter the IP address of the server, e.g: 192.168.43.245

* Second, choose an operation. There are:

        - 1: To post the model parameters for sensors AD
        - 2: To post the model parameters for network AD
        - 3: To activate or disactivate the model
        - 4: To get the output of the ML model on the edge device
        - 5: To get the recorded sensors data
        - 6: To get the recorded network data
=================================================================

- Enter the IP address of the server:
```

Fig. 5. Cloud remote monitoring and management console.

3.4 Device Fleet Monitoring with AI

The architecture of the embedded IDS presented above is designed for a deployment on single devices, meaning that the IDS is deployed on an embedded system and analyses the data of that system only. In the context of IoT, the challenge is to monitor and to ensure security to large fleets of heterogeneous IoT devices, equipped with different sensors or different interfaces. In this case, it is of course possible to deploy the IDS on compatible devices, each one endowed with an IDS running at the edge and reporting to the central cloud server. This is necessary to provide real-time detection capabilities, but the constrained resources on the edge limit the usage of powerful AI-based detection model. However, on the server side, alerts and data from the whole fleet can be aggregated and high computation resources are available, enabling a lot of new analysis possibilities: from intrusion, anomaly or failure detection, to smart visualization and business intelligence.

Cloud IDS. Since the edge computation resources and storage are limited, it is not always possible to use cost intensive ML models at edge level. For instance, large deep neural networks sometimes require several gigabytes of memory, or rely on GPU to run in reasonable computation time. On the edge, lightweight models are sometimes preferred. However, it is possible to deploy powerful and expensive models on the server side, with the goal of verifying and confirming alerts generated on the edge side. In other words, when an alarm is generated on the edge, it is notified on the server along with some metadata and on the server side, it is analyzed a second time by the "twin" detection model. With this architecture, one can provide real-time, lightweight detection systems at the edge while fully exploiting the capabilities of AI based detection on the server side, while minimizing the amount of transmitted data.

Fleet Anomaly Detection. At server level, it also becomes possible to aggregate the alerts and other information from multiple devices to improve the security analysis. When analysing the relations of similar devices between each other, if we assume a nominal operation for the fleet of devices, we can detect devices behaviors diverging from the general tendency [15], and thereby build an anomaly detection system at fleet level. Depending on the monitored data used as input of this system, it is possible to vary the scope of detected anomalies, from attacks, missuses, environment induced variations, or failures.

Visualization and Business Intelligence. After aggregation and detection, the next use-case of fleet monitoring is smart visualization. Smart visualization should allow the user to view the fleet in a condensed way providing insight regarding what is happening and what is going to happen, in order to take action if necessary. When dealing with IoT devices, the data is heterogeneous and difficult to interpret: the edge side provides notifications from the IDS and from other components, logs and in some cases sensor values. So there is a need to aggregate this information in a form meaningful for an end user. For this purpose, AI-based dimensionality reduction have shown to be efficient [6], with algorithms like Principal Component Analysis, LLE, t-SNE and its variants, etc. Those methods reduce data in high dimension into 2-D or 3-D dimensional maps, while preserving similarities and dissimilarities of the original inputs. Dimensionality reduction can directly bring out devices with different distributions than others, thus giving hints at possible failures and providing valuable insight regarding the devices behaviour or their life-cycle (a device may for example degrade at a different pace depending on its geographical location). For the same purpose, clustering methods can be used.

3.5 Case-Studies: Automotive and Healthcare

In this sub-section we provide two similar state-of-the-art research studies that suggest similar solutions. However, with our advanced edge capabilities to monitor multiple different anomalies through sensor aggregation as well as monitoring the network for threats, we provide additional value to the existing IoT solutions or propositions.

1. **Healthcare:** The authors in [20] propose a cloud-based intelligent healthcare monitoring system that focuses on providing a smart solution to locate human organs to aid in the transplant surgical processes in the Hospitals. It is a classic approach of using IoT infrastructure in delivering life saving solutions in healthcare.
2. **Automotive:** Similarly to the approach in healthcare, as proposed in this work, the automotive industry greatly gains from the edge-to-cloud approach in the V2X infrastructure. In the paper [16], the authors, from Denso Corporation and Nanzan University in Japan, share their insights and experiences about the growing influence of cloud-based solutions in the Automotive sector. They claim that the Automotive software is evolving to become Automotive Cloud Service System (ACSS) and will continue to do so in the coming days.

4 Discussion: Other Security Services for Edge-to-Cloud

Edge devices have a life cycle like human beings. The life of an edge device starts at design, then semiconductor and Original Equipment Manufacturer (OEM) level, to pass through manufacture that will oversee feeding the device with its identity, software program, applications, and services. When the edge device is ready, it is shipped by the system maker to the market by distribution supply chains. Hence, the edge device will be able to start its mission in the field. From security viewpoint, several security services shall be considered in edge-to-cloud context. We mainly mention assets provisioning, secure firmware update over the air (SFUOTA) and device identity. Those can be seen as micro-services fully managed by a remote side that is the server. An illustration can be depicted in Fig. 6.

4.1 Assets Provisioning

An asset is any sensitive data that is used to derive or manipulate secrets. Those assets could be:

- Chip/device private asymmetric key along with signed certificate for the public key.
- Chip/device symmetric master key.
- Device unique identifier.
- Chip maker/OEM public key certificate.

We can distinguish two provisioning phases in the life cycle of an edge device: before shipping (i.e. at manufacture stage) and after shipping (i.e. in the field stage). Before shipping, the provisioning is generally made locally in a safe zone at the manufacture and not remotely. This is to reduce the risk of tampering

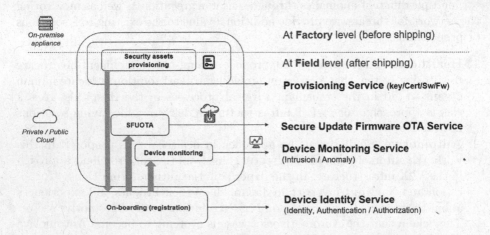

Fig. 6. Edge-to-cloud security services.

with the initial assets. Ideally, an HSM, Hardware Security Module local server, is needed to ensure a maximal security by considering a certification authority (CA) that will be the unique guardian of signing certificate, as requested from OEMs generally, and storing secret keys. Then those assets are injected to the devices through a physical access such as JTAG, on a specific machine called the tester. One other approach to be used for sake of convenience, is to map the HSM server with a remote central server to allow remote provisioning to several manufacturer distant sites. The server itself may hold an HSM server as CA. Such HSM would serve the same purposes as the local HSM. In practice, such scheme could be applied when a central site as head quarter oversees provisioning several manufacturers that he may own or not. After shipping, the edge device may need to update or revoke its assets. In that case, in-field provisioning is obviously needed. Here, the remote server shall be able to provision the edge device provided that the latter is reachable from the network. Technically, a secure channel is initiated and established by the user after properly verifying the mutual identities of both parties: the server and the edge device. Therefore, the server could generate new assets and send them to the edge device. Now, the edge device will make the Host processor handle the received assets to safely store them and send them to a secure hardware layer as TPM or SE as described previously. Besides, the remote server shall be able to revoke those assets and suspend the device's activity.

4.2 Secure Firmware Update

The edge device runs a software which is a piece of code that needs to be provisioned before shipping and then updated, similarly to the key assets. More precisely, the software, called firmware, comes packed as a binary image stored in some persistent memory like the Flash. When the device starts, it boots on an embedded code from the static memory (ROM) that allows loading the firmware. The firmware itself is composed of the system code with initial applications and services needed by the kernel image or the full operation system to work properly. Before shipping, the OEM basically needs to provision the device with the firmware. That could be performed either locally by interacting directly and simultaneously with many devices at factory/OEM level; or remotely based on a management server. Such server is necessary when the edge device is already shipped and in the wild. Such mechanism would make the life of chip makers and OEMs much easier. As a matter of fact, for automotive, the conventional situation today is to drop your car off at the repair shop to get it updated with new software version. Updating the firmware remotely is a sensitive task. For this purpose, several standardization bodies are about to push upward a unified solution. We mention for instance the IETF SUIT framework [18].

4.3 Device Identity

Before the heavy presence of connected objects in our landscape, security consisted in protecting users and their access to shared resources by ensuring their identities based on security standards. Nowadays, it has become similarly important to ensure the protection of data generated by these connected objects.

Authentication. The principle of authenticating objects is the same as authenticating users, but the technologies to be implemented are quite different. Obviously, both cases share the same objectives. Authentication is the process of verifying the identity of a user or an object by comparing the credentials provided as an input with those stored in a database. These data are called authentication factors, which form the basis of authentication protocols and methods available in the cybersecurity world. We can categorize these said methods into four types:

- Hardware: includes any physical device that stores or generates a secret key on a real time basis.
- **Memorial:** such as passwords.
- **Corporeal:** which uses the human characteristics that only the rightful user has, the example of facial recognition and biometric authentication. As far as an IoT is concerned, the equivalent of a biometric is a "PUF" (Physically Unclonable Function) [26], whose security is standardized as per ISO/IEC 20897.
- **Reactional:** includes everything that is unique, that only the user can produce, like a signature or a gesture.

Based on these methods we can distinguish between three types of authentications:

- **Mono-Factor Authentication:** which consists of using a single (factor/method) to validate both the user and the object identity.
- **Multi-Factor Authentication:** which consists of using more than one method to validate both the user and the object identity.
- **Single-Sign On (SSO) authentication:** it is a mechanism that allows the user and the object to access one or more resources at the same time without having to go through the authentication service each time.

Authorization. Authorization is the mechanism of determining whether the authenticated user can gain access to resources or perform specific actions. This function is called RBAC (Role Based Access Control), which is a security concept for managing access rights in a computerized system. Access rights are not managed by an administrator but delegated to an IAM (Identity Access Management) solution also called User-IAM that is based on authentication and authorization. The aims of an User-IAM can be applied by analogy to the Device-IAM. The difference lies in the tools and the implementation of the concept. As for IAM-Device, unique identifiers such as IMEI serial numbers, UUIDs, MAC addresses, etc., allow to establish a first level of Mono-Factor Authentication of devices. Some devices reinforce their security by storing these identifiers in secure elements in the hardware (such as in Hardware Security Modules or

HSMs, Trusted Execution Environments or TEEs, Secure Elements, etc.). However, this mono-factor authentication aspect can be improved. Like User-IAM, this mechanism can be strengthened by adding a second layer of authentication through PUF (Physically Unclonable Function). PUF is a technology that extracts a unique identifier from the intrinsic properties of each device. The output of a PUF is unique to a device and reproducible, and therefore constitutes an identifier.

Practical Use-Case. In general practice, a server-side microservice implements a standard connectivity protocol, such as Lightweight M2M (LwM2M) or FIDO device on-boarding [3]. It allows to connect the device at its first connection to authenticate and authorize it to access the server resources. More precisely, the process is realized in two phases:

- On-boarding: First, a primary server-side microservice will ask the Device to communicate its identifier. This identifier will be verified by another microservice. In a second step, the primary microservice will request the PUF image which will be compared to its exact value in a secure database in the cloud.
- Authorization: Once, and only if, the authentication is verified, the primary microservice will assign a token to the device to allow it to access the server's resources.

5 Conclusion

We propose a novel approach for anomaly and intrusion detection, based on Artificial Intelligence in the context of edge-to-cloud security monitoring. This framework is motivated by the need to provide security services, like monitoring, device identity management or secure firmware update, to fleets of IoT devices in various applications fields: automotive, healthcare, smart-homes, etc. In those ecosystems, millions of edge devices need to embed real-time security systems to prevent attacks and intrusions, all reporting to a central server. We propose to enhance such systems with machine learning-based anomaly detection methods in order to improve the detection scope and capabilities and to make an overall better usage of the complex and heterogeneous data processed at the edge. We introduce a customizable edge IDS, monitoring network interfaces and sensors to detect multiple types of threats including but not limited to fault injections, and network cyberattacks like DoS or ARP spoofing attacks. The scope of our framework extends to advanced analytics: artificial intelligence can be used at its best on the cloud server side for fleet monitoring by aggregating and correlating data from millions of devices to detect anomalies, failures, to provide smart visualizations and eventually gain valuable insight for business intelligence.

References

1. Acıiçmez, O., Schindler, W., Koç, Ç.K.: Cache based remote timing attack on the AES. In: Abe, M. (ed.) CT-RSA 2007. LNCS, vol. 4377, pp. 271–286. Springer, Heidelberg (2006). https://doi.org/10.1007/11967668_18

2. Alliance, C.S.: Matter home automation connectivity standard. https://csa-iot. org/all-solutions/matter/ (2022)
3. Alliance, F.: Fido device onboard: a specification for automated, secure IoT provisioning technology, April-2021. https://fidoalliance.org/intro-to-fido-device-onboard (2021)
4. Alliance, O.M.: Lightweight machine to machine technical specification Aug-2020. https://www.openmobilealliance.org/release/LightweightM2M/, https:// omaspecworks.org/what-is-oma-specworks/iot/lightweight-m2m-lwm2m/ (2020)
5. Barenghi, A., Breveglieri, L., Koren, I., Naccache, D.: Fault injection attacks on cryptographic devices: theory, practice, and countermeasures. Proc. IEEE **100**(11), 3056–3076 (2012). http://dblp.uni-trier.de/db/journals/pieee/pieee100. html#BarenghiBKN12
6. Bergmeir, P.: Enhanced Machine Learning and Data Mining Methods for Analysing Large Hybrid Electric Vehicle Fleets based on Load Spectrum Data. Springer, Cham (2018)
7. Criteria, C.: Common Criteria. https://www.commoncriteriaportal.org/index.cfm, https://www.commoncriteriaportal.org/index.cfm
8. Dusart, P., Letourneux, G., Vivolo, O.: Differential fault analysis on A.E.S. In: Zhou, J., Yung, M., Han, Y. (eds.) ACNS 2003. LNCS, vol. 2846, pp. 293–306. Springer, Heidelberg (2003). https://doi.org/10.1007/978-3-540-45203-4_23
9. ENISA: EUCS - Cloud Services Scheme. https://www.enisa.europa.eu/ publications/eucs-cloud-service-scheme/
10. Eurosmart: Eurosmart IoT Certification Scheme. https://www.eurosmart.com/ eurosmart-iot-certification-scheme/
11. Facon, A., et al.: High Precision EMFI Detector using Machine Learning and Sensor Fusion
12. Global Platform: Security Evaluation Standard for IoT Platforms (SESIP). Version 1.0. Document Reference: GP_FST_070 (2020)
13. Goodfellow, I.J., Shlens, J., Szegedy, C.: Explaining and harnessing adversarial examples. arXiv preprint arXiv:1412.6572 (2014)
14. Hardt, D.: The OAuth 2.0 Authorization Framework. RFC 6749 (2012). https:// doi.org/10.17487/RFC6749,https://www.rfc-editor.org/info/rfc6749
15. Hendrickx, K.: A general anomaly detection framework for fleet-based condition monitoring of machines. Mech. Syst. Signal Process. **139**, 106585 (2020)
16. Iwai, A., Aoyama, M.: Automotive cloud service systems based on service-oriented architecture and its evaluation. In: 2011 IEEE 4th International Conference on Cloud Computing, pp. 638–645. IEEE (2011)
17. Krasovsky, A., Maro, E.: Actual and historical state of side channel attacks theory, pp. 1–7 (2019). https://doi.org/10.1145/3357613.3357627
18. Moran, B., Tschofenig, H., Brown, D., Meriac, M.: A Firmware Update Architecture for Internet of Things. Internet-Draft draft-ietf-suit-architecture-12, Internet Engineering Task Force, https://datatracker.ietf.org/doc/draft-ietf-suit-architecture/12/, work in Progress
19. NIST-USA: Federal information processing standard 140–3. https://csrc.nist.gov/ publications/detail/fips/140/3/final
20. Parane, K.A., Patil, N.C., Poojara, S.R., Kamble, T.S.: Cloud based intelligent healthcare monitoring system. In: 2014 International Conference on Issues and Challenges in Intelligent Computing Techniques (ICICT), pp. 697–701. IEEE (2014)

21. Perianin, T., Carré, S., Dyseryn, V., Facon, A., Guilley, S.: End-to-end automated cache-timing attack driven by machine learning. J. Crypt. Eng. 11(2), 135–146 (2021)
22. PSA: PSA Certified. https://www.psacertified.org/getting-certified/
23. Qiu, P., Wang, D., Lyu, Y., Qu, G.: Voltjockey: breaking SGX by software-controlled voltage-induced hardware faults. In: 2019 Asian Hardware Oriented Security and Trust Symposium (AsianHOST), pp. 1–6 (2019). https://doi.org/10.1109/AsianHOST47458.2019.9006701
24. Sabt, M., Achemlal, M., Bouabdallah, A.: Trusted execution environment: what it is, and what it is not. In: 2015 IEEE Trustcom/BigDataSE/ISPA, vol. 1, pp. 57–64 (2015). https://doi.org/10.1109/Trustcom.2015.357
25. Shahid, M.R., Blanc, G., Zhang, Z., Debar, H.: Anomalous communications detection in IoT networks using sparse autoencoders. In: 2019 IEEE 18th International Symposium on Network Computing and Applications (NCA), pp. 1–5. IEEE (2019)
26. Shamsoshoara, A., Korenda, A., Afghah, F., Zeadally, S.: A survey on physical unclonable function (puf)-based security solutions for internet of things December-2020. https://www.sciencedirect.com/science/article/pii/S1389128620312275 (2020)
27. Shelby, Z., Hartke, K., Bormann, C.: The constrained application protocol (CoAP)(RFC 7252) Jun-2014. http://www.rfc-editor.org/info/rfc7252 (2014)
28. Standard, O.: MQTT version 5.0 Jun-2019. https://mqtt.org/mqtt-specification/ (2019)
29. The OpenSSL Project: OpenSSL: The open source toolkit for SSL/TLS (2003). www.openssl.org

A New Addition Law in Twisted Edwards Curves on Non Local Ring

Moha Ben Taleb Elhamam[1], Abdelhakim Chillali[2](✉), and Lhoussain El Fadil[1]

[1] Sidi Mohamed Ben Abdellah University, FSDM, Fez, Morocco
[2] Sidi Mohamed Ben Abdellah University, FP, LSI, Taza, Morocco
abdelhakim.chillali@usmba.ac.ma

Abstract. Let $\mathbb{F}_q$ be a finite field of q elements with $q = p^r$ for some odd prime integer p and a positive integer r. Let $R = \mathbb{F}_q[e]$, where $e^2 = e$. The purpose of this paper is to investigate $E_{E,a,d}(R)$ be the twisted Edwards curves over R, with $a, d \in R$. In the end of the paper, we study the complexity of this new addition law in $E_{E,a,d}(R)$ and highlight some links of our results with elliptic curves cryptosystem.

Keywords: Twisted Edwards curves · Addition law · Cryptography

1 Introduction

The use of elliptic curves in cryptography is an important tool in several cryptography going back independently to Koblitz [10] and Miller [11]. Elliptic curve cryptography (ECC) is an approach to public-key cryptography based on the algebraic structure of elliptic curves over finite fields. It allows smaller keys to provide equivalent security compared to other cryptosystem. It can also be used to encrypt images of different sizes in embedded systems such as in (cf. [12–14]). In particular, it is shown that Edwards curves and twisted Edwards curves can be very useful to improve the efficiency of protocols (cf. [1–4]). Let us quote here some interesting works that are related to the subject of our paper. In 2007, Edwards introduced a new normal form for elliptic curves on a field K with characteristic an odd prime p, containing a unified addition formula for adding and doubling points (cf. [1]). Bernstein and Lange, presented fast explicit formulas for group operations on an Edwards curve and they compared it to the different shapes of elliptic curves and different coordinate systems for base group operations. The comparison indicated that the Edwards curve is a good choice in cryptography (cf. [2]).

Thereafter, in 2008, Bernstein and his co-authors introduced the twisted Edwards curves with equation:

$$(aX^2 + Y^2)Z^2 = Z^4 + dX^2Y^2. \tag{1}$$

For $Z \neq 0$ the homogeneous point $(X : Y : Z)$ represents the affine point $(X/Z, Y/Z)$ of equation: $aX^2 + Y^2 = 1 + dX^2Y^2$, where $a, d \in K$ are non zero

A. Nitaj and K. Zkik (Eds.): I4CS 2022, CCIS 1747, pp. 40–53, 2022.
https://doi.org/10.1007/978-3-031-23201-5_3

and distinct. In addition, they introduced explicit formulas for addition and doubling over a finite field K as follows:

$$(X_1, Y_1) + (X_2, Y_2) = \left(\frac{X_1 Y_2 + Y_1 X_2}{1 + d X_1 X_2 Y_1 Y_2}, \frac{Y_1 Y_2 - a X_1 X_2}{1 - d X_1 X_2 Y_1 Y_2} \right),$$

the group operations on Edwards curves were faster than those of most other elliptic curve models known at the time. The mentioned authors gave quick explicit formulas for twisted Edwards curves in projective and inverted coordinates. Furthermore, they showed that twisted Edwards curves save more times than many other curves (cf. [3]). In the same year, Bernstein and his co-authors introduced the binary Edwards curves (cf. [5]). In 2019, Boudabra and Nitaj studied the twisted Edwards curves on the finite field $\mathbb{F}_p$ where $p \geq 5$ is a prime number, and they extend their study to the ring $\mathbb{Z}/p^r\mathbb{Z}$ and $\mathbb{Z}/p^r q^s\mathbb{Z}$. They also proposed a new scheme and studied its efficiency and security (cf. [4]). In the current work, we study twisted Edwards curves over the ring $R = \mathbb{F}_q[e]$, with $e^2 = e$ and $\mathbb{F}_q$ the finite field of order $q = p^n$, n a positive integer, and p an odd prime integer. Furthermore, we give the relation between twisted Edwards curves over a finite field $\mathbb{F}_q$ and twisted Edwards curves over the ring R. In 2022, Elhamam and his co-authors studied the binary Edwards curves on the ring $\mathbb{F}_{2^n}[e]$, $e^2 = e$ (cf. [8]). This paper is structured as follows: In Sect. 2, we collect some known arithmetic properties of the ring R which we need to use in the remainder. In Sect. 3, we define the twisted Edwards curves $E_{E,a,d}(R)$ over R and study the invertibility of $ab(a-b)$ in R, which allows us to define the two twisted Edwards curves $E_{E,\pi_0(a),\pi_0(d)}(\mathbb{F}_q)$ and $E_{E,\pi_1(a),\pi_1(d)}(\mathbb{F}_q)$, where π_0 and π_1 are two surjective morphisms of rings defined by:

$$\pi_0 : \begin{array}{c} \mathbb{F}_q[e] \rightarrow \mathbb{F}_q \\ x_0 + x_1 e \mapsto x_0 \end{array} \quad \text{and} \quad \pi_1 : \begin{array}{c} \mathbb{F}_q[e] \rightarrow \mathbb{F}_q \\ x_0 + x_1 e \mapsto x_0 + x_1. \end{array}$$

Next, we present the elements of $E_{a,d}(R)$ and give a bijection between the two sets; $E_{E,a,d}(R)$ and $E_{E,\pi_0(a),\pi_0(d)}(\mathbb{F}_q) \times E_{E,\pi_1(a),\pi_1(d)}(\mathbb{F}_q)$. Section 4 is dedicated to the study of the addition in twisted Edwards curves over the ring R. We define the additive law $P \tilde{+} Q$ in $E_{E,a,d}(R)$ by $P \tilde{+} Q = \tilde{\pi}^{-1}(\tilde{\pi}(P) + \tilde{\pi}(Q))$, for all points P and Q of $E_{E,a,d}(R)$, and we conclude that the map $\tilde{\pi}$ is an isomorphism between the groups $E_{E,a,d}(R)$ and $E_{E,\pi_0(a),\pi_0(d)}(\mathbb{F}_q) \times E_{E,\pi_1(a),\pi_1(d)}(\mathbb{F}_q)$. Thereafter, we study the complexity of the sum law in the twisted Edwards curve $E_{E,a,d}(R)$. We conclude by highlighting some links of our results with cryptography. For more works in this direction we refer the reader to [7, 9].

2   The Ring $\mathbb{F}_q[e]$, $e^2 = e$

Let $\mathbb{F}_q$ be a finite field with $q = p^r$ for some odd prime integer p and a positive integer r. Consider the quotient ring $R = \frac{\mathbb{F}_q[X]}{X^2 - X}$. Since $X^2 - X$ is the minimal polynomial of e over $\mathbb{F}_q$, the ring R is identified to the ring $\mathbb{F}_q[e]$, where $e^2 = e$. Therefore,

$$R = \{x_0 + x_1 e | (x_0, x_1) \in (\mathbb{F}_q)^2\}.$$

The arithmetic operations in R can be decomposed into operations in $\mathbb{F}_q$ and they are computed as follows:

$$X + Y = (x_0 + y_0) + (x_1 + y_1)e,$$
$$X \cdot Y = (x_0 y_0) + (x_0 y_1 + x_1 y_0 + x_1 y_1)e.$$

Then we have the following known proprieties [6] :

1. $(R, +, \cdot)$ is a finite unitary commutative ring.
2. R is an $\mathbb{F}_q$-vector space of dimension 2 with $\mathbb{F}_q$-basis $\{1, e\}$.
3. $X \cdot Y = (x_0 y_0) + ((x_0 + x_1)(y_0 + y_1) - x_0 y_0)e$.
4. $X^2 = x_0^2 + ((x_0 + x_1)^2 - x_0^2)e$.
5. $X^3 = x_0^3 + ((x_0 + x_1)^3 - x_0^3)e$.
6. Put $X = x_0 + x_1 e \in R$. Then, X is invertible in R if and only if $x_0 \neq 0$ and $x_0 + x_1 \neq 0$. In this case we have, $X^{-1} = x_0^{-1} + ((x_0 + x_1)^{-1} - x_0^{-1})e$.
7. R is a non local ring.
8. π_0 and π_1 are two surjective morphisms of rings.

In the remainder of this paper we *assume that* $p \neq 2$.

3   Twisted Edwards Curves over the Ring R

Let X, Y, a and d be four elements of R such that $X = x_0 + x_1 e$, $Y = y_0 + y_1 e$, $a = a_0 + a_1 e$ and $d = d_0 + d_1 e$. We recall that a twisted Edwards curve is defined over finite fields. By analogous, we extend it as follows:

Definition 1. *A twisted Edwards curve is defined over R is defined by the equation:*

$$aX^2 + Y^2 = 1 + dX^2 Y^2$$

such that $\Delta = ad(a - d)$ is invertible in R. We denote it by $E_{E,a,d}(R)$;

$$E_{E,a,d}(R) := \{(X, Y) \in R \mid aX^2 + Y^2 = 1 + dX^2 Y^2\}.$$

The following proposition allows to test the inversibility of Δ.

Proposition 1. *Let $\Delta_0 = a_0 d_0 (a_0 - d_0)$ and $\Delta_1 = (a_0 + a_1)(d_0 + d_1)((a_0 + a_1) - (d_0 + d_1))$. Then,*

$$\Delta = \Delta_0 + (\Delta_1 - \Delta_0) \, and \begin{cases} \Delta_0 = \pi_0(\Delta) \\ \Delta_1 = \pi_1(\Delta). \end{cases}$$

Proof. We have:

$\Delta = ad(a - d)$

$= (a_0 + a_1 e)(d_0 + d_1 e)((a_0 + a_1 e) - (d_0 + d_1 e))$

$= [a_0 d_0 + (a_0 d_1 + a_1 d_0 + a_1 d_1)e][(a_0 - d_0) + (a_1 - d_1)e]$

$= a_0 d_0 (a_0 - d_0) + [a_0 d_0 (a_1 - d_1) + (a_0 d_1 + a_1 d_0 + a_1 d_1)(a_0 - d_0) + (a_0 d_1 + a_1 d_0 + a_1 d_1)(a_1 - d_1)]e$

$= a_0 d_0 (a_0 - d_0) + [(a_0 + a_1)(d_0 + d_1)((a_0 + a_1) - (d_0 + d_1)) - a_0 d_0 (a_0 - d_0)]e$

$= \Delta_0 + (\Delta_1 - \Delta_0)e.$

Thus, $\Delta_0 = \pi_0(\Delta)$ and $\Delta_1 = \pi_1(\Delta)$.   □

The following corollary is an immediate consequence of Proposition 1.

Corollary 1. Δ *is invertible in* R *if and only if* $\Delta_0 \neq 0$ *and* $\Delta_1 \neq 0$.

By Corollary 1, if Δ is invertible in R, then $E_{E,\pi_0(a),\pi_0(d)}(\mathbb{F}_q)$ and $E_{E,\pi_1(a),\pi_1(d)}(\mathbb{F}_q)$ are two twisted Edwards curves over the finite field $\mathbb{F}_q$. Note that

$$E_{E,\pi_0(a),\pi_0(d)}(\mathbb{F}_q) = \{(x,y) \in (\mathbb{F}_q)^2 \mid a_0 x^2 + y^2 = 1 + d_0 x^2 y^2\},$$
$$E_{E,\pi_1(a),\pi_1(d)}(\mathbb{F}_q) = \{(x,y) \in (\mathbb{F}_q)^2 \mid (a_0 + a_1)x^2 + y^2 = 1 + (d_0 + d_1)x^2 y^2\}.$$

The following theorem characterizes the points of the twisted Edwards curves.

Theorem 1. *Let* X *and* Y *be two elements of* R. $(X, Y) \in E_{E,a,d}(R)$ *if and only if* $(\pi_i(X), \pi_i(Y)) \in E_{E,\pi_i(a),\pi_i(d)}(\mathbb{F}_q)$, *for* $i \in \{0, 1\}$.

Proof. We have:

$$aX^2 + Y^2 = (a_0 + a_1 e)(x_0 + x_1 e)^2 + (y_0 + y_1 e)^2$$
$$= (a_0 + a_1 e)(x_0^2 + ((x_0 + x_1)^2 - x_0^2)e) + y_0^2 + ((y_0 + y_1)^2 - y_0^2)e$$
$$= a_0 x_0^2 + y_0^2 + [(a_0 + a_1)(x_0 + x_1)^2 + (y_0 + y_1)^2 - a_0 x_0^2 - y_0^2]e, \text{ and}$$

$$1 + dX^2 Y^2 = 1 + (d_0 + d_1 e)(x_0 + x_1 e)^2 (y_0 + y_1 e)^2$$
$$= 1 + (d_0 + d_1 e)(x_0^2 + ((x_0 + x_1)^2 - x_0^2)e)(y_0^2 + ((y_0 + y_1)^2 - y_0^2)e)$$
$$= 1 + d_0 x_0^2 y_0^2 + [(d_0 + d_1)(x_0 + x_1)^2 (y_0 + y_1)^2 - d_0 x_0^2 y_0^2]e,$$

As $\{1, e\}$ is an $\mathbb{F}_q$-basis of the $\mathbb{F}_q$-vector space R, then $aX^2 + Y^2 = 1 + dX^2 Y^2$ if and only if

$$\begin{cases} a_0 x_0^2 + y_0^2 = 1 + d_0 x_0^2 y_0^2 \\ \text{and} \\ (a_0 + a_1)(x_0 + x_1)^2 + (y_0 + y_1)^2 = 1 + (d_0 + d_1)(x_0 + x_1)^2 (y_0 + y_1)^2 \end{cases}.$$

Which gives the result. $\square$

Corollary 2. *The mapping:*

$$\tilde{\pi}_i : E_{E,a,d}(R) \rightarrow E_{E,\pi_i(a),\pi_i(d)}(\mathbb{F}_q)$$
$$(X, Y) \mapsto (\pi_i(X), \pi_i(Y))$$

is well defined, $i \in \{0, 1\}$.

Proof. By Theorem 1, we have $(\pi_i(X), \pi_i(Y)) \in E_{E,\pi_i(a),\pi_i(d)}(\mathbb{F}_q)$. If $(X_1, Y_1) = (X_2, Y_2)$, then $X_2 = X_1$ and $Y_2 = Y_1$. Therefore,

$$\tilde{\pi}_i(X_2, Y_2) = (\pi_i(X_2), \pi_i(Y_2))$$
$$= (\pi_i(X_1), \pi_i(Y_1))$$
$$= \tilde{\pi}_i(X_1, Y_1).$$

$\square$

Now we classify the elements of $E_{E,a,d}(R)$. In fact we have:

Proposition 2. *The elements of $E_{E,a,d}(R)$ are of the form:*

- (X, Y) *such that X is invertible,*
- $(xe, \alpha + ye)$ *such that $\alpha \in \{-1, 1\}$ and $(x, \alpha + y) \in E_{E,\pi_1(a),\pi_1(d)}(\mathbb{F}_q)$,*
- $(x - xe, y + (\alpha - y)e)$ *such that $\alpha \in \{-1, 1\}$ and $(x, y) \in E_{E,\pi_0(a),\pi_0(d)}(\mathbb{F}_q)$.*

Proof. Let $P = (X, Y) \in E_{E,a,d}(R)$, where $X = x_0 + x_1 e$ and $Y = y_0 + y_1 e$. We distinguish two cases of X:

The First case: X is invertible.

The second case: X is not invertible. In this case we distinguish the next two sub-cases:

i) If $X = xe$, where $x \in \mathbb{F}_q$, we have: $\pi_0(xe, y_0 + y_1 e) = (0, y_0) \in E_{E,\pi_0(a),\pi_0(d)}(\mathbb{F}_q)$ then, $(0, y_0) = (0, 1)$ or $(0, y_0) = (0, -1)$, so $(xe, Y) = (xe, \alpha + ye)$ such that $(x, \alpha + y) \in E_{E,\pi_1(a),\pi_1(d)}(\mathbb{F}_q)$; $\alpha \in \{-1, 1\}$.

ii) If $X = x - xe$, where $x \in \mathbb{F}_q$, then we have: $\pi_1(x - xe, y_0 + y_1 e) = (0, y_0 + y_1) \in E_{E,\pi_1(a),\pi_1(d)}(\mathbb{F}_q)$ then, $(0, y_0 + y_1) = (0, 1)$ or $(0, y_0 + y_1) = (0, -1)$, so $(x - xe, Y) = (x - xe, y + (\alpha - y)e)$ such that $(x, y) \in E_{E,\pi_0(a),\pi_0(d)}(\mathbb{F}_q)$; $\alpha \in \{-1, 1\}$.

$\square$

Corollary 3. *The maps $\tilde{\pi}_0$ and $\tilde{\pi}_1$ are surjective.*

Proof. Let $(x, y) \in E_{E,\pi_0(a),\pi_0(d)}(\mathbb{F}_q)$ (resp. $(x', y') \in E_{E,\pi_1(a),\pi_1(d)}(\mathbb{F}_q)$), then $(x - xe, y + (1 - y)e)$ (resp. $(x'e, 1 + (y' - 1)e)$) is an antecedent of (x, y) (resp. (x', y')). $\square$

The following theorem establishes a $1 - 1$ correspondence between $E_{E,a,d}(R)$ and $E_{E,\pi_0(a),\pi_0(d)}(\mathbb{F}_q) \times E_{E,\pi_1(a),\pi_1(d)}(\mathbb{F}_q)$, and so it will be used to calculate the cardinal of $E_{E,a,d}(R)$ in Corollary 4.

Theorem 2. *The map $\tilde{\pi}$ defined by:*

$$\tilde{\pi} : E_{E,a,d}(R) \to E_{E,\pi_0(a),\pi_0(d)}(\mathbb{F}_q) \times E_{E,\pi_1(a),\pi_1(d)}(\mathbb{F}_q)$$
$$(X, Y) \mapsto ((\pi_0(X), \pi_0(Y)), (\pi_1(X), \pi_1(Y)))$$

is a bijection.

Proof.

- As $\tilde{\pi}_0$ and $\tilde{\pi}_1$ are well defined, then $\tilde{\pi}$ is well defined.

- Let $((x_0, y_0), (x_1, y_1)) \in E_{E,\pi_0(a),\pi_0(d)}(\mathbb{F}_q) \times E_{E,\pi_1(a),\pi_1(d)}(\mathbb{F}_q)$, then

$$a_0 x_0^2 + y_0^2 = 1 + d_0 x_0^2 y_0^2,$$

$$(a_0 + a_1)x_1^2 + y_1^2 = 1 + (d_0 + d_1)x_1^2 y_1^2,$$

Put $X = x_0 + (x_1 - x_0)e$ and $Y = y_0 + (y_1 - y_0)e$. We have:

$$aX^2 + Y^2 = a_0 x_0^2 + y_0^2 + [(a_0 + a_1)x_1^2 + y_1^2 - a_0 x_0^2 - y_0^2]e,$$
$$1 + dX^2Y^2 = 1 + d_0 x_0^2 y_0^2 + [(d_0 + d_1)x_1^2 y_1^2 - d_0 x_0^2 y_0^2]e,$$

So $(X, Y) \in E_{E,a,d}(R)$. Note that $\tilde{\pi}((x_0 + (x_1 - x_0)e, y_0 + (y_1 - y_0)e)) = ((x_0, y_0), (x_1, y_1))$. Hence $\tilde{\pi}$ is a surjective map.

- Let (X, Y) and (X', Y') are elements of $E_{E,a,d}(R)$, where $X = x_0 + x_1 e$, $Y = y_0 + y_1 e$, $X' = x_0' + x_1' e$, $Y' = y_0' + y_1' e$. If $(x_0, y_0) = (x_0', y_0')$ and $(x_0 + x_1, y_0 + y_1) = (x_0' + x_1', y_0' + y_1')$, then

$$\begin{cases} x_0' = x_0 \\ y_0' = y_0 \end{cases} \text{ and } \begin{cases} x_1' = x_1 \\ y_1' = y_1. \end{cases}$$

Therefore, $\tilde{\pi}$ is an injective application.

We can easily show that the mapping $\tilde{\pi}^{-1}$ defined by:

$$\tilde{\pi}^{-1}((x_0, y_0), (x_1, y_1)) = (x_0 + (x_1 - x_0)e, y_0 + (y_1 - y_0)e)$$

is the converse of $\tilde{\pi}$.

□

Corollary 4. *The cardinal of $E_{E,a,d}(R)$ equals to the cardinal of $E_{E,\pi_0(a),\pi_0(d)}(\mathbb{F}_q) \times E_{E,\pi_1(a),\pi_1(d)}(\mathbb{F}_q)$.*

Example 1. In $R = \mathbb{F}_5[e]$, let $a = 1 + 3e$ and $d = 2 + 3e$. We have:

$E_{E,a,d}(R) = \{(0, 1), (0, 4), (0, 1 + 3e), (0, 4 + 2e), (2, 2 + 3e), (2, 3 + 2e), (3, 2 + 3e), (3, 3 + 2e),$

$(2e, 1 + 4e), (2e, 4 + e), (3e, 1 + 4e), (3e, 4 + e), (1 + 4e, e), (1 + 4e, 4e),$

$(2 + e, 2 + 3e), (2 + e, 3 + 2e), (2 + 3e, 2 + 2e), (2 + 3e, 2 + 4e), (2 + 3e, 3 + 3e),$

$(2 + 3e, 3 + e), (3 + 4e, 2 + 3e), (3 + 4e, 3 + 2e), (1 + e, 0), (4 + e, e),$

$(4 + e, 4e), (1 + 2e, 0), (3 + 2e, 2 + 2e), (3 + 2e, 2 + 4e), (3 + 2e, 3 + 3e),$

$(3 + 2e, 3 + e), (4 + 3e, 0), (4 + 4e, 0)\},$

$E_{E,\pi_0(a),\pi_0(d)}(\mathbb{F}_5) = \{(0, 1), (0, 4), (1, 0), (2, 2), (2, 3), (3, 2), (3, 3), (4, 0)\},$

$E_{E,\pi_1(a),\pi_1(d)}(\mathbb{F}_5) = \{(0, 1), (0, 4), (2, 0), (3, 0)\}.$

4 Addition in Twisted Edwards Curve $E_{E,a,d}(R)$

Let (x_1, y_1), (x_2, y_2) two points on the twisted Edwards curve $E_{E,\pi_i(a),\pi_i(d)}(\mathbb{F}_q)$, for $i \in \{0, 1\}$.

The sum of these points on $E_{E,\pi_i(a),\pi_i(d)}(\mathbb{F}_q)$, for $i \in \{0, 1\}$ is given by:

$$(x_1, y_1) + (x_2, y_2) = \left(\frac{x_1 y_2 + y_1 x_2}{1 + \pi_i(d)x_1 x_2 y_1 y_2}, \frac{y_1 y_2 - \pi_i(a)x_1 x_2}{1 - \pi_i(d)x_1 x_2 y_1 y_2} \right). \tag{2}$$

The neutral element of this law is $(0, 1)$ and the inverse of an element (x_1, y_1) is $(-x_1, y_1)$. These formulas are complete if $\pi_i(a)$ is a square and $\pi_i(d)$ is a non-square in the field $\mathbb{F}_q$, for $i \in \{0, 1\}$ (cf. [3]).

Lemma 1. *Let $a = a_0 + a_1e$ be an element the R. Then, a is a square in R if and only if a_0 and $a_0 + a_1$ are squares in $\mathbb{F}_q$.*

Proof. Let us start by proving the direct implication. If a is a square in R, then there exists $b = b_0 + b_1e \in R$, with $a = b^2$. Thus, $a_0 + a_1e = b_0^2 + ((b_0 + b_1)^2 - b_0^2)e$. So $a_0 = b_0^2$ and $a_1 = (b_0 + b_1)^2 - b_0^2$. Therefore, $a_0 = b_0^2$ and $a_0 + a_1 = (b_0 + b_1)^2$, i.e. a_0 and $a_0 + a_1$ are squares in $\mathbb{F}_q$.

For the converse let $a = a_0 + a_1e$ be an element of R, with a_0 and $a_0 + a_1$ are squares in $\mathbb{F}_q$. Then, there exists $(b_0, b_1) \in (\mathbb{F}_q)^2$, where $a_0 = b_0^2$ and $a_0 + a_1 = b_1^2$. Therefore, $a_0 + a_1e = b_0^2 + (b_1^2 - b_0^2)e = (b_0 + (b_1 - b_0)e)^2$, i.e. $a_0 + a_1e$ is a square in R. □

The following example shows that if a is not a square in R, then the addition on $E_{E,a,d}(R)$ is not always defined as in the following example. Consider $p = 5$, $a = 2 + 3e$, $d = 2 + 3e$, then a and d are not squares and $P = (2 + 4e, 1)$ and $Q = (4, 4 + 2e)$ are a point on $E_{E,a,d}(R)$. Nevertheless, $P + Q$ not possible since the inverse of $1 + dX_1X_2Y_1Y_2 = e$ does not exist.

Lemma 2. *Let $d_0 + d_1e$, $\alpha \in \{-1, 1\}$, and (X_1, Y_1), (X_2, Y_2) be two points of the twisted Edwards curve $E_{E,a,d}(R)$, where $X_1 = x_0 + x_1e$, $Y_1 = y_0 + y_1e$, $X_2 = x_0' + x_1'e$ and $Y_1 = y_0' + y_1'e$, then $\alpha + dX_1X_2Y_1Y_2$ is invertible in R if and only if $\alpha + d_0x_0x_0'y_0y_0' \neq 0$ and $\alpha + (d_0 + d_1)(x_0 + x_1)(x_0' + x_1')(y_0 + y_1)(y_0' + y_1') \neq 0$ in $\mathbb{F}_q$.*

Proof. We have:

$$\alpha + dX_1X_2Y_1Y_2 = \alpha + (d_0 + d_1e)(x_0 + x_1e)(x_0' + x_1'e)(y_0 + y_1e)(y_0' + y_1'e)$$
$$= \alpha + d_0x_0x_0'y_0y_0' + [\alpha + (d_0 + d_1)(x_0 + x_1)(x_0' + x_1')(y_0 + y_1)(y_0' + y_1') -$$
$$(\alpha + d_0x_0x_0'y_0y_0')]e,$$

$\alpha + dX_1X_2Y_1Y_2$ is invertible in R if and only if $\pi_0(\alpha + dX_1X_2Y_1Y_2) \neq 0$ and $\pi_1(\alpha + dX_1X_2Y_1Y_2) \neq 0$ in $\mathbb{F}_q$, i.e.: $\alpha + d_0x_0x_0'y_0y_0' \neq 0$ and $\alpha + (d_0 + d_1)(x_0 + x_1)(x_0' + x_1')(y_0 + y_1)(y_0' + y_1') \neq 0$ in $\mathbb{F}_q$. □

Corollary 5. *Let $d_0 + d_1e$ be an element in R and (X_1, Y_1), (X_2, Y_2) two points of the twisted Edwards curve $E_{E,a,d}(R)$. If $\pi_0(d)$ and $\pi_1(d)$ are not a square in $\mathbb{F}_q$, then $\alpha + dX_1X_2Y_1Y_2$ is invertible in R, $\alpha \in \{-1, 1\}$.*

Corollary 6. *Let a, d be two elements of R and (X_1, Y_1), (X_2, Y_2) two points of the twisted Edwards curve $E_{E,a,d}(R)$. Assume that a is a squre and d is not a square in R, then*

$$(X_1, Y_1) + (X_2, Y_2) = \left(\frac{X_1Y_2 + Y_1X_2}{1 + dX_1X_2Y_1Y_2}, \frac{Y_1Y_2 - aX_1X_2}{1 - dX_1X_2Y_1Y_2}\right)$$

is well defined in $E_{E,a,d}(R)$.

In order to reduce the computation cost in $E_{E,a,d}(R)$, we introduce a new addition in $E_{E,a,d}(R)$ in Sect. 4, and we compare the computation cost of the new law with the that law given in Corollary 6.

As $\tilde{\pi}$ is a bijection mapping between the two sets $E_{E,a,d}(R)$ and $E_{E,\pi_0(a),\pi_0(d)}(\mathbb{F}_q) \times E_{E,\pi_1(a),\pi_1(d)}(\mathbb{F}_q)$, we can define the sum on $E_{E,a,d}(R)$.

Definition 2. *Let $P = (X_1, Y_1)$ and $Q = (X_2, Y_2)$ be two points of the twisted Edwards curve $E_{E,a,d}(R)$, assume that a is a square and d is not a square in R, we define the additive law $P \tilde{+} Q$ in $E_{E,a,d}(R)$ by: $P \tilde{+} Q = \tilde{\pi}^{-1}(\tilde{\pi}(P) + \tilde{\pi}(Q))$.*

Keep the assumptions of the above definition during this section. The following corollaries can be easily proved:

Corollary 7. *The set $(E_{E,a,d}(R), \tilde{+})$ is a commutative group, which has $(0, 1)$ as its zero element and the inverse of (X_1, Y_1) is $(-X_1, Y_1)$.*

Corollary 8. *The $\tilde{\pi}$ mapping is an isomorphism of groups.*

By using formula (2), Theorem 2 and Proposition 2, we shall give the explicit formula of sum of two points in the twisted Edwards curve $E_{E,a,d}(R)$ in the next lemmas.

Lemma 3. *Let $P = (xe, \alpha + ye)$ and $Q = (x'e, \beta + y'e)$ be two elements of $E_{E,a,d}(R)$ such that $\alpha \in \{-1, 1\}$ and $\beta \in \{-1, 1\}$. Then $P \tilde{+} Q = (x_3 e, \alpha\beta + (y_3 - \alpha\beta)e)$, where*

$$x_3 = \frac{x(\beta + y') + (\alpha + y)x'}{1 + \pi_1(d)xx'(\alpha + y)(\beta + y')} \text{ and } y_3 = \frac{(\alpha + y)(\beta + y') - \pi_1(a)xx'}{1 - \pi_1(d)xx'(\alpha + y)(\beta + y')}.$$

Proof. As $\begin{cases} \tilde{\pi}_0(xe, \alpha + ye) = (0, \alpha) \\ \tilde{\pi}_0(x'e, \beta + y'e) = (0, \beta) \end{cases}$ and $\begin{cases} \tilde{\pi}_1(xe, \alpha + ye) = (x, \alpha + y) \\ \tilde{\pi}_1(x'e, \beta + y'e) = (x', \alpha + y') \end{cases}$,

according to the formula (2), we have:

$\tilde{\pi}_0(xe, \alpha + ye) + \tilde{\pi}_0(x'e, \beta + y'e) = (0, \alpha\beta)$ and $\tilde{\pi}_1(xe, \alpha + ye) + \tilde{\pi}_1(x'e, \beta + y'e) = (x_3, y_3)$, where

$$x_3 = \frac{x(\beta + y') + (\alpha + y)x'}{1 + \pi_1(d)xx'(\alpha + y)(\beta + y')} \text{ and } y_3 = \frac{(\alpha + y)(\beta + y') - \pi_1(a)x'}{1 - \pi_1(d)xx'(\alpha + y)(\beta + y')}.$$

Therefore,

$$P \tilde{+} Q = \tilde{\pi}^{-1}((0, \alpha\beta), (x_3, y_3)) = (x_3 e, \alpha\beta + (y_3 - \alpha\beta)e).$$

$\square$

Lemma 4. *Let $P = (xe, \alpha + ye)$ and $Q = (x' - x'e, y' + (\beta - y')e)$ be two points of the twisted Edwards curve $E_{E,a,d}(R)$ such that $\alpha \in \{-1, 1\}$ and $\beta \in \{-1, 1\}$. Then $P \tilde{+} Q = (\alpha x' + (\beta x - \alpha x')e, \alpha y' + (\beta(\alpha + y) - \alpha y')e)$.*

Proof. As $\begin{cases} \tilde{\pi}_0(xe, \alpha + ye) = (0, \alpha) \\ \tilde{\pi}_0(x' - x'e, y' + (\beta - y')e) = (x', y') \end{cases}$ and $\begin{cases} \tilde{\pi}_1(xe, \alpha + ye) = (x, \alpha + y) \\ \tilde{\pi}_1(x' - x'e, y' + (\beta - y')e) = (0, \beta) \end{cases}$,

According to the formula (2), we have:

$$\tilde{\pi}_0(xe, \alpha + ye) + \tilde{\pi}_0(x'e, \beta + y'e) = (\alpha x', \alpha y') \text{ and } \tilde{\pi}_1(xe, \alpha + ye) + \tilde{\pi}_1(x'e, \beta + y'e) = (\beta x, \beta(\alpha + y)).$$

Then

$$P\tilde{+}Q = \tilde{\pi}^{-1}((\alpha x', \alpha y'), (\beta x, \beta(\alpha + y))) = (\alpha x' + (\beta x - \alpha x')e, \alpha y' + (\beta(\alpha + y) - \alpha y')e).$$

$\square$

Lemma 5. *Let* $P = (x - xe, y + (\alpha - y)e)$ *and* $Q = (x' - x'e, y' + (\beta - y')e)$ *be two points of the twisted Edwards curve* $E_{E,a,d}(R)$ *such that* $\alpha \in \{-1, 1\}$ *and* $\beta \in \{-1, 1\}$. *Then* $P\tilde{+}Q = (x_3 - x_3e, y_3 + (\alpha\beta - y_3)e)$, *where*

$$x_3 = \frac{xy' + yx'}{1 + \pi_0(d)xx'yy'} \text{ and } y_3 = \frac{yy' - \pi_0(a)xx'}{1 - \pi_0(d)xx'yy'}.$$

Proof. As $\begin{cases} \tilde{\pi}_0(x - xe, y + (\alpha - y)e) = (x, y) \\ \tilde{\pi}_0(x' - x'e, y' + (\beta - y')e) = (x', y') \end{cases}$ and $\begin{cases} \tilde{\pi}_1(x - xe, y + (\alpha - y)e) = (0, \alpha) \\ \tilde{\pi}_1(x' - x'e, y' + (\beta - y')e) = (0, \beta) \end{cases}$,

According to formula (2), we have:

$$\tilde{\pi}_0(x - xe, y + (\alpha - y)e) + \tilde{\pi}_0(x' - x'e, y' + (\beta - y')e) = (x_3, y_3) \text{ and}$$
$$\tilde{\pi}_1(x - xe, y + (\alpha - y)e) + \tilde{\pi}_1(x' - x'e, y' + (\beta - y')e) = (0, \alpha\beta), \text{ where}$$

$$x_3 = \frac{xy' + yx'}{1 + \pi_0(d)xx'yy'} \text{ and } y_3 = \frac{yy' - \pi_0(a)xx'}{1 - \pi_0(d)xx'yy'}.$$

Therefore,

$$P\tilde{+}Q = \tilde{\pi}^{-1}((x_3, y_3), (0, \alpha\beta)) = (x_3 - x_3e, y_3 + (\alpha\beta - y_3)e).$$

$\square$

Lemma 6. *Let* $P = (xe, \alpha + ye)$ *and* $Q = (x_0 + x_1e, y_0 + y_1e)$ *be two points of the twisted Edwards curve* $E_{E,a,d}(R)$ *such that* $\alpha \in \{-1, 1\}$. *Then* $P\tilde{+}Q = (\alpha x_0 + (x_3 - \alpha x_0)e, \alpha y_0 + (y_3 - \alpha y_0)e)$, *where*

$$x_3 = \frac{x(y_0 + y_1) + (\alpha + y)(x_0 + x_1)}{1 + \pi_1(d)x(x_0 + x_1)(\alpha + y)(y_0 + y_1)} \text{ and } y_3 = \frac{(\alpha + y)(y_0 + y_1) - \pi_1(a)x(x_0 + x_1)}{1 - \pi_1(d)x(x_0 + x_1)(\alpha + y)(y_0 + y_1)}.$$

Proof. As $\begin{cases} \tilde{\pi}_0(xe, \alpha + ye) = (0, \alpha) \\ \tilde{\pi}_0(x_0 + x_1e, y_0 + y_1e) = (x_0, y_0) \end{cases}$ and $\begin{cases} \tilde{\pi}_1(xe, \alpha + ye) = (x, \alpha + y) \\ \tilde{\pi}_1(x_0 + x_1e, y_0 + y_1e) = (x_0 + x_1, y_0 + y_1) \end{cases}$,

According to the formula (2), we have:

$$\tilde{\pi}_0(xe, \alpha + ye) + \tilde{\pi}_0(x_0 + x_1e, y_0 + y_1e) = (\alpha x_0, \alpha y_0) \text{ and}$$
$$\tilde{\pi}_1(xe, \alpha + ye) + \tilde{\pi}_1(x_0 + x_1e, y_0 + y_1e) = (x_3, y_3), \text{ where}$$

$$x_3 = \frac{x(y_0 + y_1) + (\alpha + y)(x_0 + x_1)}{1 + \pi_1(d)x(x_0 + x_1)(\alpha + y)(y_0 + y_1)} \text{ and } y_3 = \frac{(\alpha + y)(y_0 + y_1) - \pi_1(a)x(x_0 + x_1)}{1 - \pi_1(d)x(x_0 + x_1)(\alpha + y)(y_0 + y_1)}.$$

Therefore,

$$P \tilde{+} Q = \tilde{\pi}^{-1}((\alpha x_0, \alpha y_0), (x_3, y_3)) = (\alpha x_0 + (x_3 - \alpha x_0)e, \alpha y_0 + (y_3 - \alpha y_0)e).$$

$\square$

Lemma 7. *Let* $P = (x - xe, y + (\alpha - y)e)$ *and* $Q = (x_0 + x_1 e, y_0 + y_1 e)$ *be two points of the twisted Edwards curve* $E_{E,a,d}(R)$ *such that* $\alpha \in \{-1, 1\}$. *Then* $P \tilde{+} Q = (x_3 + (\alpha(x_0 + x_1) - x_3)e, y_3 + (\alpha(y_0 + y_1) - y_3)e)$, *where*

$$x_3 = \frac{xy_0 + x_0 y}{1 + \pi_0(d)xx_0 y y_0} \text{ and } y_3 = \frac{yy_0 - \pi_1(a)xx_0}{1 - \pi_1(d)xx_0 y y_0}.$$

Proof. As $\begin{cases} \tilde{\pi}_0(x - xe, y + (\alpha - y)e) = (x, y) \\ \tilde{\pi}_0(x_0 + x_1 e, y_0 + y_1 e) = (x_0, y_0) \end{cases}$ and $\begin{cases} \tilde{\pi}_1(x - xe, y + (\alpha - y)e) = (0, \alpha) \\ \tilde{\pi}_1(x_0 + x_1 e, y_0 + y_1 e) = (x_0 + x_1, y_0 + y_1) \end{cases}$,

According to the formula (2), we have:

$$\tilde{\pi}_0(x - xe, y + (\alpha - y)e) + \tilde{\pi}_0(x_0 + x_1 e, y_0 + y_1 e) = (x_3, y_3) \text{ and}$$

$$\tilde{\pi}_1(xe, \alpha + ye) + \tilde{\pi}_1(x_0 + x_1 e, y_0 + y_1 e) = (\alpha(x_0 + x_1), \alpha(y_0 + y_1)), \text{ where}$$

$$x_3 = \frac{xy_0 + x_0 y}{1 + \pi_0(d)xx_0 y y_0} \text{ and } y_3 = \frac{yy_0 - \pi_1(a)xx_0}{1 - \pi_1(d)xx_0 y y_0}.$$

Therefore,

$$P \tilde{+} Q = \tilde{\pi}^{-1}((x_3, y_3), (\alpha(x_0 + x_1), \alpha(y_0 + y_1))) = (x_3 + (\alpha(x_0 + x_1) - x_3)e, \alpha y_0 + (\alpha(y_0 + y_1) - y_3)e).$$

$\square$

Lemma 8. *Let* $P = (x_0 + x_1 e, y_0 + y_1 e)$ *and* $Q = (x_0' + x_1' e, y_0' + y_1' e)$ *be two points of the twisted Edwards curve* $E_{E,a,d}(R)$. *Then* $P \tilde{+} Q = (x_3 + (x_3' - x_3)e, y_3 + (y_3' - y_3)e)$, *where*

$$x_3 = \frac{x_0 y_0' + x_0' y_0}{1 + \pi_0(d)x_0 y_0' x_0' y_0}, y_3 = \frac{y_0 y_0' - \pi_0(a)x_0 x_0'}{1 - \pi_0(d)x_0 y_0' x_0' y_0},$$

$$x_3' = \frac{(x_0 + x_1)(y_0' + y_1') + (y_0 + y_1)(x_0' + x_1')}{1 + \pi_1(d)(x_0 + x_1)(y_0' + y_1')(y_0 + y_1)(x_0' + x_1')}$$

and

$$y_3' = \frac{(y_0 + y_1)(y_0' + y_1') - \pi_1(a)(x_0 + x_1)(x_0' + x_1')}{1 - \pi_1(d)(x_0 + x_1)(y_0' + y_1')(y_0 + y_1)(x_0' + x_1')}.$$

Proof. As $\begin{cases} \tilde{\pi}_0(x_0 + x_1 e, y_0 + y_1 e) = (x_0, y_0) \\ \tilde{\pi}_0(x_0' + x_1' e, y_0' + y_1' e) = (x_0', y_0') \end{cases}$ and $\begin{cases} \tilde{\pi}_1(x_0 + x_1 e, y_0 + y_1 e) = (x_0 + x_1, y_0 + y_1) \\ \tilde{\pi}_1(x_0' + x_1' e, y_0' + y_1' e) = (x_0' + x_1', y_0' + y_1') \end{cases}$,

According to the formula (2), we have:

$$\tilde{\pi}_0(x_0 + x_1 e, y_0 + y_1 e) + \tilde{\pi}_0(x_0' + x_1' e, y_0' + y_1' e) = (x_3, y_3) \text{ and}$$

$$\tilde{\pi}_1(x_0 + x_1e, y_0 + y_1e) + \tilde{\pi}_1(x_0' + x_1'e, y_0' + y_1'e) = (x_3', y_3'), \text{ where}$$

$$x_3 = \frac{x_0 y_0' + x_0' y_0}{1 + \pi_0(d)x_0 y_0' x_0' y_0}, y_3 = \frac{y_0 y_0' - \pi_0(a)x_0 x_0'}{1 - \pi_0(d)x_0 y_0' x_0' y_0},$$

$$x_3' = \frac{(x_0 + x_1)(y_0' + y_1') + (y_0 + y_1)(x_0' + x_1')}{1 + \pi_1(d)(x_0 + x_1)(y_0' + y_1')(y_0 + y_1)(x_0' + x_1')} \text{ and}$$
$$y_3' = \frac{(y_0 + y_1)(y_0' + y_1') - \pi_1(a)(x_0 + x_1)(x_0' + x_1')}{1 - \pi_1(d)(x_0 + x_1)(y_0' + y_1')(y_0 + y_1)(x_0' + x_1')}.$$

Therefore,

$$P \tilde{+} Q = \tilde{\pi}^{-1}((x_3, y_3), (x_3', y_3')) = (x_3 + (x_3' - x_3)e, y_3 + (y_3' - y_3)e),$$

which completes the proof.   □

Lemmas 3, 4, 5, 6, 7 and 8 can be regrouped in the next theorem which given the additive law of the twisted Edwards curve $E_{E,a,d}(R)$.

Theorem 3. *Let $P = (X_1, Y_1)$ and $Q = (X_2, Y_2)$ be in $E_{E,a,d}(R)$. Assume that $\pi_i(a)$ is a square and $\pi_i(d)$ is not a square in $\mathbb{F}_q$, where $i \in \{0, 1\}$. Under the law $\tilde{+}$, $(E_{E,a,d}(R), \tilde{+})$ is an Abelian group with zero element $(0, 1)$. More precisely for every $\alpha, \beta \in \{-1, 1\}$, we have $P \tilde{+} Q = (X_3, Y_3)$ is given by:*

1) If $\tilde{\pi}_0(P) = (0, \alpha)$, then

$$X_3 = \alpha\pi_0(X_2) + (x_3 - \alpha\pi_0(X_2))e,$$
$$Y_3 = \alpha\pi_0(Y_2) + (y_3 - \alpha\pi_0(Y_2))e,$$

where
$$\tilde{\pi}_1(P) + \tilde{\pi}_1(Q) = (x_3, y_3).$$

2) If $\tilde{\pi}_1(P) = (0, \alpha)$, then

$$X_3 = x_3 + (\alpha\pi_1(X_2) - x_3)e,$$
$$Y_3 = y_3 + (\alpha\pi_1(Y_2) - y_3)e,$$

where
$$\tilde{\pi}_0(P) + \tilde{\pi}_0(Q) = (x_3, y_3).$$

3) If $\tilde{\pi}_0(P) = (0, \alpha)$ and $\tilde{\pi}_1(Q) = (0, \beta)$, then

$$X_3 = \alpha\pi_0(X_2) + (\beta\pi_1(X_1) - \alpha\pi_0(X_2))e,$$
$$Y_3 = \alpha\pi_0(Y_2) + (\beta\pi_1(Y_1) - \alpha\pi_0(Y_2))e.$$

4) If $\tilde{\pi}_0(P) \neq (0, \alpha)$ and $\tilde{\pi}_1(P) \neq (0, \alpha)$, then

$$X_3 = x_3 + (x_3' - x_3)e,$$
$$Y_3 = y_3 + (y_3' - y_3)e,$$

where

$$\tilde{\pi}_0(P) + \tilde{\pi}_0(Q) = (x_3, y_3),$$
$$\tilde{\pi}_1(P) + \tilde{\pi}_1(Q) = (x_3', y_3').$$

Proof. For the proof, we can easily show that the lemmas from 3 to 8 verify the cases of the theorem.

□

Now we shall focus on the complexity of the sum law in the twisted Edwards curve $E_{E,a,d}(R)$.

Let S be the cost of the sum and M the cost of the multiplication in the field $\mathbb{F}_q$. The computation cost of calculating $P + Q$ the sum that is defined in Corollary 6 and $P \tilde{+} Q$ the sum that is defined in Definition 2 are given in the following table (Table 1):

Table 1. The complexity of the additions in the twisted Edwards curve $E_{E,a,d}(R)$.

Addition	+		$\tilde{+}$	
Cost	Sum	Mult	Sum	Mult
Lemma 3	21S	75M	13S	13M
Lemma 4	3S	7M	2S	4M
Lemma 5	7S	27M	5S	13M
Lemma 6	41S	146M	13S	13M
Lemma 7	12S	32M	6S	13M
Lemma 8	48S	284M	26S	26M

The following graphics illustrate the above results (Fig. 1).

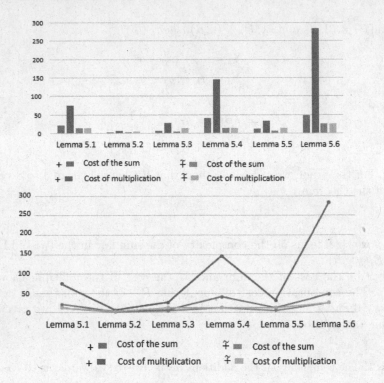

Fig. 1. The complexity of the additions in the twisted Edwards curve $E_{E,a,d}(R)$.

Concerning the complexity reduction of the sum law in the twisted Edwards curve $E_{E,a,d}(R)$, one can remark that the direct calculation of the sum $P + Q$ is more expensive compared to the calculation of this sum $P \tilde{+} Q$ using the isomorphism $\tilde{\pi}$. Which explain the need of this study.

Links with Cryptography

Let us close this section with few applications in cryptography. We have:

- $card(E_{E,a,d}(R)) = card(E_{E,\pi_0(a),\pi_0(d)}(\mathbb{F}_q)) \times card(E_{E,\pi_1(a),\pi_1(d)}(\mathbb{F}_q))$.
- $E_{E,a,d}(R)$ and $E_{E,\pi_0(a),\pi_0(d)}(\mathbb{F}_q) \times E_{E,\pi_1(a),\pi_1(d)}(\mathbb{F}_q)$ have the same security discrete logarithm problem.
- In cryptanalysis, break the discrete logarithm problem on $E_{E,a,d}(R)$ is equivalent to break the discrete logarithm problem on $E_{E,\pi_0(a),\pi_0(d)}(\mathbb{F}_q)$ and $E_{E,\pi_1(a),\pi_1(d)}(\mathbb{F}_q)$.

References

1. Harold Edwards, M.: Normal form for elliptic curves. Bull. Am. Math. Soc. **44**(03), 393–423 (2007)

2. Bernstein, D.J., Lange, T.: Faster addition and doubling on elliptic curves. In: Kurosawa, K..(ed.) ASIACRYPT 2007. LNCS, vol. 4833, pp. 29–50. Springer, Heidelberg (2007). https://doi.org/10.1007/978-3-540-76900-2_3

3. Bernstein, D.J., Birkner, P., Joye, M., Lange, T., Peters, C.: Twisted Edwards curves. In: Vaudenay, S. (ed.) AFRICACRYPT 2008. LNCS, vol. 5023, pp. 389–405. Springer, Heidelberg (2008). https://doi.org/10.1007/978-3-540-68164-9_26

4. Boudabra, M., Nitaj, A.: A new public key cryptosystem based on Edwards curves. J. Appl. Math. Comput. **61**(1), 431–450 (2019). https://doi.org/10.1007/s12190-019-01257-y

5. Bernstein, D.J., Lange, T., Rezaeian Farashahi, R.: Binary Edwards curves. In: Oswald, E., Rohatgi, P. (eds.) CHES 2008. LNCS, vol. 5154, pp. 244–265. Springer, Heidelberg (2008). https://doi.org/10.1007/978-3-540-85053-3_16

6. Boulbot, A., Chillali, A., Mouhib, A.: Elliptic curves over the ring R. Bol. Soc. Paran. **38**(3), 193–201 (2020)

7. Elhamam, M.B.T., Chillali, A., El Fadil, L., Twisted Hessian curves over the Ring $\mathbb{F}_q[e], e^2 = e$. Bol. Soc. Paran. **40** (2022). https://doi.org/10.52699/bspm.15867

8. Elhamam, M.B.T., Chillali, A., El Fadil, L.: Public key cryptosystem and binary Edwards curves on the ring $\mathbb{F}_{2^n}[e], e^2 = e$ for data management. In: 2nd International Conference on Innovative Research in Applied Science, Engineering and Technology (IRASET), pp. 1–4 (2022). https://doi.org/10.1109/IRASET52964.2022.9738249

9. Elhamam, M.B.T., Chillali, A., Grini, A., El Fadil, L.: El Gamal cryptosystem on a montgomery curves over non local ring. In: WSEAS Transactions on Mathematics, E-ISSN: 2224–2880, V. 21 (2022). https://doi.org/10.37394/23206.2022.21.13

10. Koblitz, N., Elliptic curve cryptosystems. Math. Comput. **48**(177), 203–209 (1987). https://doi.org/10.2307/2007884

11. Miller, V.S.: Use of elliptic curves in cryptography. In: Williams, H.C. (ed.) CRYPTO 1985. LNCS, vol. 218, pp. 417–426. Springer, Heidelberg (1986). https://doi.org/10.1007/3-540-39799-X_31

12. Chillali, S., Oughdir, L.: ECC image encryption using matlab simulink blockset. In: Motahhir, S., Bossoufi, B. (eds.) ICDTA 2021. LNNS, vol. 211, pp. 835–846. Springer, Cham (2021). https://doi.org/10.1007/978-3-030-73882-2_76

13. Chillali, S., Oughdir, L.: ECC Image Encryption Using System Generator. J. Theor. Appl. Inf. Technol. **100**(15), 5419 542515 (2022)

14. Chillali, S., Oughdir, L.: Construction of a matrix by an elliptic curve for image encryption. Int. J. Emerg. Technol. Adv. Eng. **12**(09), 122–129 (2022)

Contributed Papers

New Lattice-Based Signature Based on Fiat-Shamir Framework Without Aborts

Chik How Tan[iD] and Theo Fanuela Prabowo[(✉)][iD]

Temasek Laboratories, National University of Singapore, Singapore, Singapore
{tsltch,tsltfp}@nus.edu.sg

Abstract. Recently, a number of side-channel attacks were launched on lattice-based signatures based on "Fiat-Shamir with aborts". This shows that signature based on Fiat-Shamir with aborts is vulnerable to side-channel attacks. In this paper, we construct a lattice-based signature scheme based on Fiat-Shamir framework without aborts, and instantiate it over NTRU lattices. The proposed signature is proved to be secure in the random oracle model under some newly defined problems. We also prove the hardness of these new problems and show that the search RLWE problem is as hard as these newly defined problems. The public key size, secret key size and signature size of the proposed signature scheme are 1920 bytes, 512 bytes and 4096 bytes respectively for 180-bit quantum security level. The key and signature sizes of the proposed signature are comparable to those of the currently known signatures, such as, Dilithium, Falcon, qTESLA, MLS, BCM and MITAKA.

1 Introduction

There are two generic frameworks to construct signature, that are, hash-and-sign constructions and Fiat-Shamir framework [17] constructions. The hash-and-sign construction requires some trapdoor functions, while Fiat-Shamir framework construction does not necessarily use trapdoor function. In lattice-based signature, there are a number of signatures constructed based on Fiat-Shamir framework [17], for example, Lyubashevsky signature [26], Dilithium [13], qTESLA [4] and BCM [6]. Due to the original Fiat-Shamir framework for lattices being subjected to statistical attacks, Lyubashevsky introduced a technique with aborts to make signature independent of the secret key against statistical attack for recovering the secret key. Since then, numerous practically efficient lattice based signatures based on "Fiat-Shamir with aborts" were proposed. These include Lyubashevsky [27], Dilithium [13], qTESLA [4] and BCM [6].

Although lattice-based signatures based on "Fiat-Shamir with aborts" is secure against statistical attack, it is subjected to side channel attacks, for example, fault attacks [9,15,33] on qTESLA and Dilithium respectively, power analysis attack [23] on Dilithium, electromagnetic attack [22] on Falcon etc. The attacks exploit the aborts condition to generate a valid signature that will leak

A. Nitaj and K. Zkik (Eds.): I4CS 2022, CCIS 1747, pp. 57–76, 2022.
https://doi.org/10.1007/978-3-031-23201-5_4

the secret key. In [6], Behnia, et al. introduced a method for removing one rejection sampling condition in signature generation. This reduced the number of aborts when generating signature, but it still keeps the same secret key in signature generation. In this paper, we construct new lattice-based signature that eliminates the use of rejection sampling, that is, Fiat-Shamir without aborts. Our approach is different from that of [4,6,13,27] which fixed secret key for signature generation. Our idea is to change the secret key as ephemeral secret key in each signature generation. Hence, this resists statistical attack as the statistical attack required a fixed secret key in signature generation. The proposed signature uses the trapdoor function in NTRU lattices as long term secret key that enable us to have an ephemeral secret key that is dependent on and different from the long term secret key. The public key size, secret key size and signature size of the proposed signature are 1920 bytes, 512 bytes and 4096 bytes respectively for 180-bit quantum security level. The key and signature sizes of the proposed signature scheme are comparable to those of the currently known signatures, such as, Dilithium [13], Falcon [18], qTESLA [4], MLS [12], BCM [6] and MITAKA [16] schemes.

The organization of this paper is as follows. In Sect. 2, we provide a brief review on lattices and BKZ algorithm, as well as setup some notations that will be used throughout this paper. In Sect. 3, we define some useful distributions that will be used to construct a signature. In Sect. 4, we define some new problems on lattices and showed that the search RLWE problem is as hard as these newly defined problems. These new problems will be used to prove that the proposed signature is secure against existential forgery under adaptive chosen message attack in the random oracle model. In Sect. 5, we give a brief definition of signature schemes and propose a new lattice based signature which is instantiated over NTRU lattices. In Sect. 6, we give detailed security proof for the proposed signature under random oracle model. In Sect. 7, we examine the public/secret key size and signature size for various security levels. Finally, we conclude the paper in Sect. 8.

2   Preliminaries

2.1   Notations

Let n be a power of 2 and q be odd prime; and $q_1 = \frac{q-1}{2}$ throughout this paper.

Rings. Let $\mathbb{Z}_q = \mathbb{Z}/q\mathbb{Z}$ denote the quotient ring of integers modulo q, and let $\mathcal{R}$, $\mathcal{R}_q$ denote the rings $\mathbb{Z}[x]/(x^n + 1)$ and $\mathbb{Z}_q[x]/(x^n + 1)$ respectively. Denote $\mathcal{R}_q^* = \{a(x) \in \mathcal{R}_q \mid a(x) \text{ is invertible}\}$.

For a polynomial $\bar{\mathbf{a}}(x) = \bar{a}_0 + \bar{a}_1 x + \cdots + \bar{a}_{n-1} x^{n-1} \in \mathcal{R}$, define $\mathbf{a}(x) = \sum_{i=0}^{n-1} a_i x^i$ where $a_i = \bar{a}_i \bmod q = \begin{cases} a_i & \text{if } a_i \leq q_1, \\ a_i - q & \text{otherwise} \end{cases}$. So, $a_i \in [-q_1, q_1]$. We denote its vector form as $\mathbf{a} = (a_0, a_1, \cdots, a_{n-1})$. We also denote the vector form of $a(x)b(x) \in \mathcal{R}_q$ as $\mathbf{ab}$.

Euclidean and Infinity Norm. Given $a(x) = a_0 + a_1 x + \cdots + a_{n-1} x^{n-1} \in \mathcal{R}$, define the Euclidean norm as $\| \mathbf{a} \| = \sqrt{\sum_{i=0}^{n-1} a_i^2}$ and the infinity norm as $\| \mathbf{a} \|_\infty = \max_i \{ | a_i | \}$. The length of $\mathbf{a}$ is defined as its Euclidean norm $\| \mathbf{a} \|$.

Distribution. Let $t < n$ be a positive integer and $t_1 = \lfloor \frac{n}{3} \rfloor$.

(1) Distribution $X_{t,n}$ on $\{-1, 0, 1\}$, defined by $\Pr[X_{t,n} = 1 \text{ or} -1] = \frac{t}{n}$ and $\Pr[X_{t,n} = 0] = \frac{n-t}{n}$.

(2) Distribution set $\mathcal{E}_t := \{ \mathbf{z} = (z_1, \cdots, z_n) \in \mathcal{R}_q \mid z_i \leftarrow X_{t,n} \text{ for } i = 1, \cdots, n \}$.

(3) Distribution $Y_{t_1,n}$ on $\{-1, 0, 1\}$, defined by $\Pr[Y_{t_1,n} = 1] = \frac{t_1+1}{n}$, $\Pr[Y_{t_1,n} = -1] = \frac{t_1}{n}$, and $\Pr[Y_{t_1,n} = 0] = \frac{n-2t_1-1}{n}$.

(4) Distribution set $\mathcal{F}_{t_1} := \{ \mathbf{z} = (z_1, \cdots, z_n) \in \mathcal{R}_q \mid z_i \leftarrow Y_{t_1,n} \text{ for } i = 1, \cdots, n \}$.

(5) Distribution χ_σ: A distribution χ with standard deviation σ.

(6) Normal Distribution: Denote as $\mathcal{N}(0, \sigma^2)$ with mean 0 and standard deviation σ.

(7) Uniform Distribution on $[-K, K]$: Denote as $\mathcal{U}_K$ with mean 0 and standard deviation $\sqrt{\frac{K(K+1)}{3}}$.

(8) $z \leftarrow \chi_\sigma$: z is drawn from distribution χ_σ.

(9) Distribution set $\mathcal{N}_\sigma^n := \{ \mathbf{z} = (z_1, \cdots, z_n) \in \mathcal{R}_q \mid z_i \leftarrow \mathcal{N}(0, \sigma^2) \text{ for } i = 1, \cdots, n \}$.

(10) Distribution set $\mathcal{BN}_{\sigma, B, \varepsilon} := \{ \mathbf{z} \in \mathcal{N}_\sigma^n \mid \|\mathbf{z}\|_\infty \leq B \}$ such that $\Pr[\mathbf{z} \in \mathcal{N}_\sigma^n \mid \|\mathbf{z}\|_\infty > B] < \varepsilon$, where $B < q_1$.

(11) $\mathcal{D}_K := \{ \mathbf{a} \in \mathcal{R}_q \mid \|\mathbf{a}\|_\infty \leq K \}$, where $K < q_1$.

2.2 Lattices and BKZ Algorithm

In this section, we give a brief review on lattices and hard problems in lattices. We first give a formal definition of lattices as follows.

Definition 1. *Let $\mathcal{B} = \{\mathbf{b}_1, \cdots, \mathbf{b}_d\} \subset \mathbb{R}^d$ be a set of d linearly independent vectors. Define a lattice $\mathcal{L}(\mathcal{B})$ generated by $\mathbf{b}_1, \cdots, \mathbf{b}_d$ as the set*

$$\mathcal{L}(\mathcal{B}) := \left\{ \sum_{i=1}^d x_i \mathbf{b}_i \mid x_i \in \mathbb{Z}, i = 1, \cdots, d \right\}.$$

The set of vectors $\mathcal{B} = \{\mathbf{b}_1, \cdots, \mathbf{b}_d\}$ is called a basis of the lattice $\mathcal{L}(\mathcal{B})$.

A basis $\mathcal{B}$ can be represented as a matrix $\mathbf{B} = [\mathbf{b}_1, \cdots, \mathbf{b}_d]^T \in \mathbb{R}^{d \times d}$ having the basis as its row vectors. Then $\mathcal{L}(\mathcal{B}) = \{\mathbf{xB} \mid \mathbf{x} \in \mathbb{Z}^d\}$, $\mathcal{L}(\mathbf{B})$ also uses to denote the lattice $\mathcal{L}(\mathcal{B})$. The determinant of a lattice $\mathcal{L}(\mathbf{B})$ is defined as

$$\det(\mathcal{L}(\mathbf{B})) = |\det(\mathbf{B})| = \sqrt{|\det(\mathbf{B}^T \mathbf{B})|}.$$

Note that the determinant of a lattice does not depend on the choice of the basis $\mathcal{B}$. The determinant of $\mathcal{L}(\mathbf{B})$ is also called the volume of a lattice $\mathcal{L}(\mathbf{B})$

as $\mathrm{Vol}(\mathcal{L}(\mathbf{B})) = |\det(\mathbf{B})|$. The length of a vector $\mathbf{v} = (v_1, \cdots, v_d) \in \mathbb{R}^d$ is the Euclidean norm of $\mathbf{v}$ and defined as $\|\mathbf{v}\| := \sqrt{\sum_{i=1}^{d} v_i^2}$. A non-zero vector in a lattice $\mathcal{L}(\mathcal{B})$ with the minimum Euclidean norm is called the shortest vector of the lattice.

The problem of finding the shortest non-zero lattice vector is called the shortest vector problem (SVP). It is known to be NP-hard under randomized reduction [1]. So far, the best algorithm to find shortest vector in a lattice is by Blockwise-Korkine-Zolotarev (BKZ) algorithm [10, 34], which is a generalization of the LLL algorithm [25]. The BKZ algorithm takes a basis $\mathbf{b}_1, \cdots, \mathbf{b}_d$ of dimension d as an input and proceeds by solving SVP on lattices of dimension $\beta < d$ using either sieving or enumeration. If the basis $\mathcal{B}^*$ is BKZ-reduced, then the computed short vector in BKZ algorithm [10] is based on the following assumptions.

Assumption 1 (Root Hermite factor δ).

$$\delta = ((\pi\beta)^{\frac{1}{\beta}} \cdot \frac{\beta}{2\pi e})^{\frac{1}{2(\beta-1)}}.$$

Assumption 2. *Let $\mathcal{B}^* = \{\mathbf{b}_1^*, \cdots, \mathbf{b}_d^*\}$ be a BKZ-reduced basis, then*

$$\|\mathbf{b}_1^*\| = \delta^d \cdot \mathrm{Vol}(\mathcal{L}(\mathcal{B}^*))^{1/d}.$$

Assumption 3 (Geometric Series Assumption). *Let $\{\mathbf{b}_1^*, \cdots, \mathbf{b}_d^*\}$ be a BKZ-reduced basis, then $\|\mathbf{b}_i^*\| = \delta^{-2(i-1)}\|\mathbf{b}_1^*\|$.*

The time complexity of BKZ algorithm with block size β on a random lattice is estimated to be $2^{0.292\beta+o(\beta)}$ in classical computers [5]. With Grover speedups, the time complexity is lowered to $2^{0.265\beta+o(\beta)}$ in quantum computers [5].

2.3   Ring-Based Learning with Errors

Let $\mathcal{R}_q = \mathbb{Z}_q[x]/(x^n + 1)$. Let χ be a distribution over $\mathcal{R}_q$. For a fixed $\mathbf{s} \in \mathcal{R}_q$ such that $\mathbf{s}$ is a short vector, the RLWE-distribution is defined as follows

$$\mathcal{D}_{\mathbf{s},\chi} = \{(\mathbf{a}, \mathbf{b} = \mathbf{sa} + \mathbf{e}) \in \mathcal{R}_q \times \mathcal{R}_q \,|\, \text{random}\, \mathbf{a} \leftarrow \mathcal{R}_q, \mathbf{e} \leftarrow \chi\}.$$

Definition 2 (Search RLWE$_{\mathbf{s},\chi}$ Problem). *Given l independent samples of $RLWE_{\mathbf{s},\chi}$ instance $(\mathbf{a}_i, \mathbf{b}_i = \mathbf{sa}_i + \mathbf{e}_i) \in \mathcal{D}_{\mathbf{s},\chi}$, find $\mathbf{s} \in \mathcal{R}_q$.*

Definition 3 (Decision RLWE$_{\mathbf{s},\chi}$ Problem). *Given l independent samples $(\mathbf{a}_i, \mathbf{b}_i) \in \mathcal{R}_q \times \mathcal{R}_q$, determine whether these samples are from $\mathcal{D}_{\mathbf{s},\chi}$ or random from $\mathcal{R}_q \times \mathcal{R}_q$.*

Lyubashevsky et al. [28] showed that the search RLWE problem quantumly reduces to the decision RLWE problem. Therefore, the decision RLWE$_{\mathbf{s},\chi}$ problem is a hard problem. They also showed that $\mathcal{D}_{\mathbf{s},\chi}$ is pseudorandom.

3   Distributions

In this section, we use the notation introduced in Sect. 2.1 and examine the properties of some distributions. We first compute the mean and variance of some distributions on $\{-1, 0, 1\}$ as follows.

Lemma 1. *Let $n > t \geq 1$. Consider the distribution $X_{t.n}$ on $\{-1, 0, 1\}$ defined in Sect. 2.1. Then, the mean and variance of this distribution are 0 and $\frac{t}{n}$ respectively.*

Lemma 2. *Let n be a power of 2, $t_1 = \lfloor \frac{n}{3} \rfloor$. Consider the distribution $Y_{t_1,n}$ on $\{-1, 0, 1\}$ defined in Sect. 2.1. Then, the mean and the variance of this distribution are $\frac{1}{n}$ and $\frac{2t_1 n + n - 1}{n^2}$ respectively.*

Lemma 3. *Let $\mathcal{U}_K$ be the uniform distribution on $[-K, K]$. Then, the mean and the variance of this distribution are 0 and $\frac{K(K+1)}{3}$ respectively.*

Lemma 4. *Let U, V be independent random variables with mean $\mathbb{E}(U), \mathbb{E}(V)$ and variance $\mathbb{V}(U), \mathbb{V}(V)$. Then,*
(a) $\mathbb{E}(U \pm V) = \mathbb{E}(U) \pm \mathbb{E}(V)$ *and* $\mathbb{V}(U \pm V) = \mathbb{V}(U) + \mathbb{V}(V)$,
(b) $\mathbb{E}(UV) = \mathbb{E}(U)\mathbb{E}(V)$ *and* $\mathbb{V}(UV) = (\mathbb{V}(U) + \mathbb{E}(U)^2) \times (\mathbb{V}(V) + \mathbb{E}(V)^2) - \mathbb{E}(U)^2 \mathbb{E}(V)^2$.

Corollary 1. *Let n be a power of 2 and $t < n$ be an integer, $t_1 = \lfloor \frac{n}{3} \rfloor$. Let U, V be independent distributions $X_{t,n}$ and $Y_{t_1,n}$ on $\{-1, 0, 1\}$ respectively. Then $\mathbb{E}(UV) = 0$ and $\mathbb{V}(UV) = \frac{t(2t_1+1)}{n^2}$.*

Proof. By Lemma 1, $\mathbb{E}(U) = 0$ and $\mathbb{V}(U) = \frac{t}{n}$. By Lemma 2, $\mathbb{E}(V) = \frac{1}{n}$ and $\mathbb{V}(V) = \frac{2t_1 n + n - 1}{n^2}$. By Lemma 4 (b), it is clear that $\mathbb{E}(UV) = 0$ and we compute the variance as follows.

$$\mathbb{V}(UV) = (\frac{t}{n} + 0^2)(\frac{2t_1 n + n - 1}{n^2} + \frac{1}{n^2}) - 0 = \frac{t(2t_1 + 1)}{n^2}.$$

Now, consider the normal distribution $\mathcal{N}(0, \sigma^2)$ with mean 0 and standard deviation σ and the density function $\rho_\sigma(x) = (\frac{1}{\sqrt{2\pi\sigma^2}})e^{-\frac{x^2}{2\sigma^2}}$ for $x \in \mathbb{R}$.

Theorem 1 ([30] Theorem 2.23 (Central Limit Theorem). *Let $X_1, X_2, \cdots, X_n$ be independent and identically distributed random variables such that $\mathbb{E}(X_i) = \mu$ and $Var(X_i) = \sigma^2$. Let $\bar{X} - \sum_{i=1}^{n} X_i$. Then $(X - \mu n)$ approximates to the normal distribution $\mathcal{N}(0, n\sigma^2)$ with mean 0 and standard deviation $\sqrt{n}\sigma$.*

Corollary 2. *Let $\mathbf{u}, \mathbf{v} \in \mathcal{R}_q$ and suppose each coordinate u_i, v_i of $\mathbf{u}, \mathbf{v}$ is sampled independently from the normal distribution $\mathcal{N}(0, \sigma_u^2)$ and $\mathcal{N}(0, \sigma_v^2)$ respectively. Then each coordinate of $\mathbf{u} + \mathbf{v}$ follows $\mathcal{N}(0, \sigma^2)$, where $\sigma = \sqrt{\sigma_u^2 + \sigma_v^2}$.*

Lemma 5. *Let* $\mathbf{u}, \mathbf{v}, \mathbf{w} \in \mathcal{R}_q$ *and each coordinates* u_i, w_i *of* $\mathbf{u}$ *and* $\mathbf{w}$ *are independently distributed random variables with mean 0 and variance* $\sigma_{\mathbf{u}}^2$ *and* $\sigma_{\mathbf{w}}^2$ *respectively. Each coordinates* v_i *of* $\mathbf{v}$ *is independently distributed random variable with mean* $\mu_{\mathbf{v}}$ *and variance* $\sigma_{\mathbf{v}}^2$. *Then,*

(1) *Each coordinate of* $\mathbf{uv}$ *approximates to* $\mathcal{N}(0, \sigma^2)$, *where* $\sigma = \sqrt{n} \sigma_{\mathbf{u}} \sqrt{\sigma_{\mathbf{v}}^2 + \mu_{\mathbf{v}}^2}$,

(2) *Each coordinate of* $\mathbf{uvw}$ *approximates to* $\mathcal{N}(0, \sigma^2)$, *where* $\sigma = n \sigma_{\mathbf{u}} \sigma_{\mathbf{w}} \sqrt{\sigma_{\mathbf{v}}^2 + \mu_{\mathbf{v}}^2}$.

Proof. (1) Let $\mathbf{uv} = (s_0, \cdots, s_{n-1})$, then $s_t = \sum_{i=0}^{n-1} \pm u_i v_{n-i+t \bmod n}$. By Lemma 4(b), each $\pm u_i v_j$ follows a random variable with mean 0 and variance $\sigma_{\mathbf{u}}^2 (\sigma_{\mathbf{v}}^2 + \mu_{\mathbf{v}}^2)$. By the Central Limit Theorem, each s_t approximates to $\mathcal{N}(0, n\sigma_{\mathbf{u}}^2 (\sigma_{\mathbf{v}}^2 + \mu_{\mathbf{v}}^2))$.

(2) Let $\mathbf{uvw} = (y_0, \cdots, y_{n-1})$, then $y_j = \sum_{i=0}^{n-1} \pm s_i w_{n-i+j \bmod n}$, where s_i is as defined above in (1). It follows that y_j is a sum of n^2 terms, each of the form $\pm u_i v_j w_k$. Note that each $\pm u_i v_j w_k$ follows a random variable with mean 0 and variance $\sigma_{\mathbf{u}}^2 (\sigma_{\mathbf{v}}^2 + \mu_{\mathbf{v}}^2) \sigma_{\mathbf{w}}^2$. Thus, by the Central Limit Theorem, each y_j approximates to $\mathcal{N}(0, n^2 \sigma_{\mathbf{u}}^2 (\sigma_{\mathbf{v}}^2 + \mu_{\mathbf{v}}^2) \sigma_{\mathbf{w}}^2)$.

Lemma 6 [11]. *For* $k > 2$, $Z \sim \mathcal{N}(0, \sigma^2)$, *then*

$$\Pr[|z| > k\sigma \mid z \leftarrow Z] \leq \frac{1}{2}(e^{-k^2} + e^{-\frac{k^2}{2}}).$$

Proposition 1. *If* $\mathbf{u}, \mathbf{v} \in \mathcal{R}_q$ *such that each coordinate of* $\mathbf{u}$ *and* $\mathbf{v}$ *are independently distributed random variables with mean* $\mu_{\mathbf{u}} = 0$ *and* $\mu_{\mathbf{v}}$; *and variance* $\sigma_{\mathbf{u}}^2$ *and* $\sigma_{\mathbf{v}}^2$ *respectively. Then,* $\Pr[\|\mathbf{uv}\|_\infty \leq k\sigma] \geq 1 - \min\{\frac{n}{2}(e^{-k^2} + e^{-\frac{k^2}{2}}), 1\}$, *where* $\sigma = \sqrt{n} \sigma_{\mathbf{u}} \sqrt{\sigma_{\mathbf{v}}^2 + \mu_{\mathbf{v}}^2}$.

Proof. Let $\mathbf{uv} = \{s_0, \cdots, s_{n-1}\}$. By Lemma 5 (1), s_i approximates to $\mathcal{N}(0, \sigma^2)$, where $\sigma = \sqrt{n} \sigma_{\mathbf{u}} \sqrt{\sigma_{\mathbf{v}}^2 + \mu_{\mathbf{v}}^2}$. Let $S_i = \{|s_i| > k\sigma\}$ and $S_{max} = \{\max_{0 \leq i \leq n-1}\{|s_i|\} > k\sigma\}$. Then, $S_{max} = \bigcup_{i=0}^{n-1} S_i$. By Lemma 6, $\Pr[|s_i| > k\sigma] \leq \frac{1}{2}(e^{-k^2} + e^{-\frac{k^2}{2}})$ for $0 \leq i \leq n-1$. We have,

$$\Pr[S_{max}] = \Pr[S_0 \cup \cdots \cup S_{n-1}] \leq n \sum_{i=0}^{n-1} \Pr[S_i] \leq \min\left\{\frac{n}{2}(e^{-k^2} + e^{-\frac{k^2}{2}}), 1\right\},$$

since $\Pr[S_i] \leq \frac{1}{2}(e^{-k^2} + e^{-\frac{k^2}{2}})$. Hence,

$$\Pr[\|\mathbf{uv}\|_\infty \leq k\sigma] = 1 - \Pr[\|\mathbf{uv}\|_\infty > k\sigma] \geq 1 - \min\left\{\frac{n}{2}(e^{-k^2} + e^{-\frac{k^2}{2}}), 1\right\}.$$

Based on Lemma 5 and Proposition 1, we define the following distributions.

Definition 4. *For* $\mathbf{z} \in \mathcal{R}_q$, *we define the following distributions*

(1) $\mathcal{N}_\sigma^n = \{\mathbf{z} = (z_1, \cdots, z_n) \in \mathcal{R}_q \mid z_i \leftarrow \mathcal{N}(0, \sigma^2) \text{ for } i = 1, \cdots, n\}$.

(2) *Let* $B < q_1$ *be integer, we define the bounded distribution* $\mathcal{BN}_{\sigma, B, \varepsilon}$ *as follows*

$$\mathcal{BN}_{\sigma, B, \varepsilon} = \{\mathbf{z} \in \mathcal{N}_\sigma^n \mid \|\mathbf{z}\|_\infty \leq B\}$$

such that $\Pr[\mathbf{z} \in \mathcal{N}_\sigma^n \mid \|\mathbf{z}\|_\infty > B] < \varepsilon$.

4   NTRU Lattices and New Problems

In this section, we will define some new problems and prove that the search RLWE problem is as hard as these newly defined problems.

Definition 5. *Let $K < q_1$, we define the K-bounded set $\mathcal{D}_K$ as $\mathcal{D}_K := \{\mathbf{a} \in \mathcal{R}_q \mid \|\mathbf{a}\|_\infty \leq K\}$.*

If $K = 1$, then $\mathcal{D}_1$ consists of elements with all coordinates in $\{-1, 0, 1\}$.

Definition 6 (NTRU Problem). *The NTRU distribution $\mathcal{D}_{\mathrm{NTRU}}$ is $\mathbf{h} = \mathbf{f}^{-1}\mathbf{g} \in \mathcal{R}_q^*$, where $\mathbf{f}, \mathbf{g} \in \mathcal{R}_q^* \cap \mathcal{D}_1$. The NTRU problem is: given $\mathbf{h} \in \mathcal{D}_{\mathrm{NTRU}}$, find $\mathbf{f}, \mathbf{g}$.*

Definition 7 (Decision NTRU problem (DNTRU)). *Let $\mathcal{D}_{\mathrm{NTRU}}$ be an NTRU distribution. The decision NTRU problem is to distinguish between samples from $\mathcal{D}_{\mathrm{NTRU}}$ and random from $\mathcal{R}_q^*$. The advantage of an algorithm $\mathcal{A}$ against the DNTRU problem is defined as*

$$\mathrm{Adv}_{\mathrm{DNTRU}}(\mathcal{A}) = \Big| \Pr[\mathcal{A}(\mathbf{h} \in \mathcal{D}_{\mathrm{NTRU}}) = 1] - \Pr[\mathcal{A}(\mathbf{h} \in \mathcal{R}_q^*) = 1] \Big|.$$

In [31, page 33], Peikert showed that search $\mathrm{RLWE}_{\mathbf{s}, \chi}$ problem is at least as hard as the decision NTRU problem. This only provides the hardness upper bound for decision NTRU problem. Recently, Pellet-Mary and Stehlé [32] proved that NTRU problem is a hard problem by reduction from ideal SVP problem to an average-case search variant of the NTRU problem and then from an average-case search variant of the NTRU problem to the decision NTRU problem. Therefore, the advantage of solving DNTRU problem is negligible, i.e. $\mathrm{Adv}_{\mathrm{DNTRU}}(\mathcal{A}) \leq \varepsilon_{\mathrm{DNTRU}}$.

Definition 8 (NTRU Lattices). *Let $\mathbf{f}, \mathbf{g} \in \mathcal{R}_q^* \cap \mathcal{D}_1$. Let $\mathbf{h} = \mathbf{f}^{-1}\mathbf{g} \in \mathcal{R}_q^*$. Define NTRU lattices $\mathcal{L}$ as $\mathcal{L} := \{(\mathbf{u}, \mathbf{v}) \in \mathcal{R}_q^2 \mid \mathbf{v} = \mathbf{u}\mathbf{h} \bmod q\}$.*

Lemma 7. *Let $K < q_1$ and suppose $\mathbf{a}$ is chosen uniformly random from $\mathcal{R}_q$. Then $\Pr[\mathbf{a} \in \mathcal{D}_K] \leq (\frac{2K+1}{q})^n$.*

Proof. Let $\mathbf{a} = (a_0, \cdots, a_{n-1})$, then $\Pr[|a_i| \leq K] \leq \frac{2K+1}{q}$. Therefore, $\Pr[\mathbf{a} \in \mathcal{D}_K] \leq (\frac{2K+1}{q})^n$.

Proposition 2. *Let $b < q_1$ and $\mathbf{a} \xleftarrow{R} \mathcal{D}_b$. Then $\Pr[\mathbf{a}\mathbf{h} \in \mathcal{D}_b] \leq (\frac{2b+1}{q})^n$.*

Proof. As $\mathbf{h}$ is invertible in $\mathcal{R}_q$, if $\mathbf{a}, \mathbf{a}' \in \mathcal{R}_q$ such that $\mathbf{a}'\mathbf{h} = \mathbf{a}\mathbf{h}$, then $\mathbf{a}' = \mathbf{a}$. Hence, $|\{\mathbf{a}\mathbf{h} \mid \mathbf{a} \in \mathcal{R}_q\}| = q^n$. We also note that $|\mathcal{D}_b| = (2b+1)^n$. Hence, $\Pr[\mathbf{a}\mathbf{h} \in \mathcal{D}_b] \leq (\frac{2b+1}{q})^n$.

Definition 9 (Small Vectors Problem ($\mathrm{SmVP}_{\hat{\mathbf{h}}, K}$)). *Let $K < q_1$, given $\hat{\mathbf{h}} \in \mathcal{R}_q^*$, find $(\mathbf{u}, \mathbf{v}) \in \mathcal{R}_q \times \mathcal{R}_q$ such that $\mathbf{v} = \mathbf{u}\hat{\mathbf{h}} \in \mathcal{R}_q$ and $\mathbf{u}, \mathbf{v} \in \mathcal{D}_K$. The advantage of an adversary $\mathcal{A}$ to solve $\mathrm{SmVP}_{\hat{\mathbf{h}}, K}$ problem is defined as $\mathrm{Adv}_{\mathrm{SmVP}_{\hat{\mathbf{h}}, K}}(\mathcal{A}) = \Pr[\mathcal{A}((\mathbf{u}, \mathbf{v}) \in \mathcal{D}_K \times \mathcal{D}_K \mid \mathbf{u}\hat{\mathbf{h}} = \mathbf{v})]$.*

So far, the best known method to find such short vectors $\mathbf{u}, \mathbf{v}$ is via BKZ algorithm on the lattice $\begin{bmatrix} \mathbf{I}_n & \hat{\mathbf{h}} \\ \mathbf{0}_n & q\mathbf{I}_n \end{bmatrix}$. But, the BKZ algorithm has exponential time complexity. Therefore, SmVP seems difficult to solve and assumes to be hard.

Definition 10 (Sum of Small Vectors Problem ($\mathrm{SSV}_{\mathbf{h},K}$)). *Let $K < q_1$ and $\mathcal{BN}_{\sigma,K,\varepsilon}$ be bounded distribution set. Define the $\mathrm{SSV}_{\mathbf{h},K}$ distribution to be*

$$\mathcal{D}_{\mathrm{SSV}_{\mathbf{h},K}} = \{\mathbf{u} = \mathbf{u}' + \mathbf{u}'' \in \mathcal{D}_{2K} \mid \mathbf{u}' \in \mathcal{U}_K, \mathbf{u}'' \in \mathcal{BN}_{\sigma,K,\varepsilon},\ \mathbf{u}'\mathbf{h} \notin \mathcal{D}_K, \mathbf{u}''\mathbf{h} \in \mathcal{D}_K\}.$$

Given $\mathbf{u} = \mathbf{u}' + \mathbf{u}'' \in \mathcal{D}_{\mathrm{SSV}_{\mathbf{h},k}}$ and $\mathbf{h}$, find $(\mathbf{u}', \mathbf{u}'') \in \mathcal{D}_K \times \mathcal{D}_K$ such that $\mathbf{u}''\mathbf{h} \in \mathcal{D}_K$.

For given $\mathbf{u} = \mathbf{u}' + \mathbf{u}'' \in \mathcal{D}_{\mathrm{SSV}_{\mathbf{h},K}}$, $\mathbf{u}$ information-theoretically hides $\mathbf{u}'$ and $\mathbf{u}''$ as there are many possibilities for $\mathbf{u}'$ and $\mathbf{u}''$ for given $\mathbf{u}$.

Definition 11 (Decision Sum of Small Vector Problem ($\mathrm{DSSV}_{\mathbf{h},K}$)). *Let $K < q_1$. Given l independent samples $\mathbf{u}_i \in \mathcal{D}_{2K}$, determine whether these samples $\mathbf{u}_i$ are from the $\mathrm{SSV}_{\mathbf{h},K}$ distribution ($\mathcal{D}_{\mathrm{SSV}_{\mathbf{h},K}}$) or random from $\mathcal{D}_{2K}$. The advantage of an adversary $\mathcal{A}$ for solving $\mathrm{DSSV}_{\mathbf{h},K}$ is defined as follows.*

$$\mathrm{Adv}_{\mathrm{DSSV}_{\mathbf{h},K}}(\mathcal{A}) = \left| \Pr[\mathcal{A}(\mathbf{u} \in \mathcal{D}_{\mathrm{SSV}_{\mathbf{h},K}}] = 1) - \Pr[\mathcal{A}(\mathbf{u} \in \mathcal{D}_{2K}) = 1] \right|.$$

By substituting $\mathbf{h}$ with $\mathbf{h}^{-1}$ in the definitions above, we can similarly define $\mathrm{SSV}_{\mathbf{h}^{-1},K}$, $\mathrm{DSSV}_{\mathbf{h}^{-1},K}$ and $\mathrm{Adv}_{\mathrm{DSSV}_{\mathbf{h}^{-1},K}}(\mathcal{A})$.

Proposition 3. *The search RLWE problem is as hard as the decision SSV problem.*

Proof. Given l independent samples $\mathbf{u}_i \in \mathcal{D}_{2K}$, the decision SSV problem is to determine whether these samples $\mathbf{u}_i$ are from the $\mathrm{SSV}_{\mathbf{h},K}$ distribution ($\mathcal{D}_{\mathrm{SSV}_{\mathbf{h},K}}$) or random from $\mathcal{D}_{2K}$. We reduce this problem to the search RLWE problem. Suppose we have an oracle $\mathcal{O}$ to solve search RLWE problem with high probability. Then we have an algorithm to solve $\mathrm{DSSV}_{\mathbf{h},K}$ problem as follows. The algorithm first chooses two distributions χ_{σ_s} and χ_{σ_e}; and $\mathbf{s} \leftarrow \chi_{\sigma_s}$, where σ_s, σ_e are the standard deviation of the distributions χ_{σ_s} and χ_{σ_e} respectively. Let $\sigma_e > \sqrt{n(\sigma^2 + \sigma_u^2)}\,\sigma_f$, where σ is defined for $\mathcal{BN}_{\sigma,K,\varepsilon}$, σ_u is the standard deviation of the uniform distribution $\mathcal{U}_K$ and σ_f is the standard deviation of the distribution used to sample the coordinates of $\mathbf{f}$ and $\mathbf{g}$. Then the algorithm constructs l RLWE pairs as

$$(\mathbf{u}_i\mathbf{h}, \mathbf{u}_i\mathbf{h}\mathbf{s} + \mathbf{e}_i), \quad \text{where } \mathbf{e}_i \leftarrow \chi_{\sigma_e}$$

and give these to the search RLWE oracle $\mathcal{O}$. The oracle $\mathcal{O}$ considers the following two cases:

Case (1): $\mathbf{u}_i$ are random: Then the input to $\mathcal{O}$ are properly distributed RLWE samples with secret $\mathbf{s}$. So, the oracle $\mathcal{O}$ returns $\mathbf{s}$ with high probability and the algorithm accepts.

Case (2): $\mathbf{u}_i = \mathbf{u}_{i1} + \mathbf{u}_{i2} \in \mathcal{D}_{\mathrm{SSV_{h,K}}}$: Then $\mathbf{u}_{i1} \in \mathcal{U}_K$, $\mathbf{u}_{i2} \in \mathcal{BN}_{\sigma,K,\varepsilon}$ and consider the following

$$\begin{aligned}
\mathbf{u}_i\mathbf{h}\mathbf{s} + \mathbf{e}_i &= (\mathbf{u}_{i1}\mathbf{h} + \mathbf{u}_{i2}\mathbf{h})\mathbf{s} + \mathbf{e}_i \\
&= (\mathbf{u}_{i1}\mathbf{h} + \bar{\mathbf{u}}_{i2})\mathbf{s} + \mathbf{e}_i \text{ where } \bar{\mathbf{u}}_{i2} = \mathbf{u}_{i2}\mathbf{h} \in \mathcal{D}_K \\
&= (\mathbf{u}_{i1}\mathbf{h} + \bar{\mathbf{u}}_{i2})(\mathbf{s} + \mathbf{f}) + \mathbf{e}_i - \mathbf{u}_{i1}\mathbf{g} - \bar{\mathbf{u}}_{i2}\mathbf{f}
\end{aligned}$$

As the standard deviation of the distribution used to sample the coordinates of $\mathbf{f}$ and $\mathbf{g}$ is σ_f, then $\mathbf{u}_{i1}\mathbf{g}$ and $\bar{\mathbf{u}}_{i2}\mathbf{f}$ follows $\mathcal{N}_{\sigma_1}^n$ and $\mathbf{u}_{i1}\mathbf{g} - \bar{\mathbf{u}}_{i2}\mathbf{f}$ follows $\mathcal{N}_{\sigma_1}^n$, where $\sigma_1 = \sqrt{n(\sigma^2 + \sigma_u^2)}\,\sigma_f$. Since $\sigma_e > \sigma_1$ and χ_{σ_e} is "wider" than $\mathcal{N}_{\sigma_1}^n$, then $(\mathbf{u}_i\mathbf{h}, \mathbf{u}_i\mathbf{h}\mathbf{s} + \mathbf{e}_i)$ "information-theoretically hide" the value of $\mathbf{s}$. So, there are many possibilities for the secret and errors that are consistent with the pairs $(\mathbf{u}_i\mathbf{h}, \mathbf{u}_i\mathbf{h}\mathbf{s} + \mathbf{e}_i)$, for example, $\mathbf{s}+\mathbf{f}$ and $\mathbf{e}_i - \mathbf{u}_{i1}\mathbf{g} - \bar{\mathbf{u}}_{i2}\mathbf{f}$. Therefore, no matter how the oracle $\mathcal{O}$ works internally, even the input pairs are not properly distributed RLWE samples. So, the oracle will reject it and the algorithm will also reject it. Hence, the search RLWE oracle could be used to solve the decision SSV problem.

Definition 12 (Advance Sum of Small Vectors Problem ($\mathrm{ASSV_{h,K}}$)). Let $K < q_1$ and $\mathcal{BN}_{\sigma,K,\varepsilon}$ be bounded distribution. Define the $\mathrm{ASSV_{h,K}}$ distribution to be

$$\mathcal{D}_{\mathrm{ASSV_{h,K}}} = \{\mathbf{v} = \mathbf{e}_1\mathbf{f} + \mathbf{e}_2\mathbf{g} \in \mathcal{D}_{2K} \mid \mathbf{e}_1, \mathbf{e}_2 \in \mathcal{E}_t,\ \mathbf{f}, \mathbf{g} \in \mathcal{F}_{t_1},\ \mathbf{e}_1\mathbf{f}, \mathbf{e}_2\mathbf{g} \in \mathcal{BN}_{\sigma,K,\varepsilon},$$
$$\mathbf{e}_1\mathbf{f}\mathbf{h}, \mathbf{e}_2\mathbf{g}\mathbf{h}^{-1} \in \mathcal{D}_K,\ \mathbf{e}_1\mathbf{f}\mathbf{h}^{-1}, \mathbf{e}_2\mathbf{g}\mathbf{h} \notin \mathcal{D}_K\}.$$

Given $\mathbf{v} = \mathbf{u}' + \mathbf{u}'' \in \mathcal{D}_{\mathrm{ASSV_{h,k}}}$ *and* $\mathbf{h}$, *find* $(\mathbf{u}', \mathbf{u}'') \in \mathcal{D}_K \times \mathcal{D}_K$ *such that* $\mathbf{u}'\mathbf{h} \in \mathcal{D}_K$, $\mathbf{u}''\mathbf{h}^{-1} \in \mathcal{D}_K$ *and* $\mathbf{u}'\mathbf{h}^{-1} \notin \mathcal{D}_K$, $\mathbf{u}''\mathbf{h} \notin \mathcal{D}_K$.

Similarly, for given $\mathbf{v} = \mathbf{e}_1\mathbf{f} + \mathbf{e}_2\mathbf{g} \in \mathcal{D}_{\mathrm{ASSV_{h,K}}}$, $\mathbf{v}$ information-theoretically hides $\mathbf{e}_1\mathbf{f}$ and $\mathbf{e}_2\mathbf{g}$ as there are many possibilities of $\mathbf{e}_1\mathbf{f}$ and $\mathbf{e}_2\mathbf{g}$ for given $\mathbf{v}$.

Definition 13 (Decision Advance Sum of Small Vector Problem ($\mathrm{DASSV_{h,K}}$)). Let $K < q_1$. Given l independent samples $\mathbf{v}_i \in \mathcal{D}_{2K}$, determine whether all $\mathbf{v}_i$ are sampled from the $\mathrm{ASSV_{h,K}}$ distribution ($\mathcal{D}_{\mathrm{ASSV_{h,K}}}$) or random from $\mathcal{D}_{2K}$. The advantage of an adversary $\mathcal{A}$ is defined as follows.

$$\mathrm{Adv}_{\mathrm{DASSV_{h,K}}}(\mathcal{A}) = \Big| \Pr[\mathcal{A}(\mathbf{v} \in \mathcal{D}_{\mathrm{ASSV_{h,K}}}) = 1] - \Pr[\mathcal{A}(\mathbf{v} \in \mathcal{D}_{2K}) = 1] \Big|.$$

Proposition 4. *The search* RLWE *problem is as hard as the decision* ASSV *problem.*

Proof. Given l independent $\mathbf{v}_i \in \mathcal{D}_{2K}$, the decision ASSV problem is to determine whether these samples $\mathbf{v}_i$ are from the $\mathrm{ASSV_{h,K}}$ distribution ($\mathcal{D}_{\mathrm{ASSV_{h,K}}}$) or random from $\mathcal{D}_{2K}$. We reduce this problem to the search RLWE problem. Suppose we have an oracle $\mathcal{O}$ to solve search RLWE problem with high probability. Then we have an algorithm to solve $\mathrm{DASSV_{h,K}}$ problem as follows. The algorithm first chooses two distributions χ_{σ_s} and χ_{σ_e}; and $\mathbf{s} \leftarrow \chi_{\sigma_s}$, where σ_s, σ_e are the standard deviation of the distributions χ_{σ_s} and χ_{σ_e} respectively. Let

$\sigma_e > \sqrt{2n}\sigma\sigma_g$, where σ is defined for $\mathcal{BN}_{\sigma,K,\varepsilon}$ and σ_g is standard deviation of the distribution used to sample the coordinates of $\mathbf{g}$. Then the algorithm constructs l RLWE pair as follows:

$$(\mathbf{v}_i\mathbf{h}, \mathbf{v}_i\mathbf{hs} + \mathbf{e}_i), \quad \text{where } \mathbf{e}_i \leftarrow \chi_{\sigma_e}$$

and give these to the search RLWE oracle $\mathcal{O}$. The oracle $\mathcal{O}$ considers the following two cases:

Case (1): $\mathbf{v}_i$ are random: Then the input to $\mathcal{O}$ are properly distributed RLWE samples with secret $\mathbf{s}$. So, the oracle $\mathcal{O}$ returns $\mathbf{s}$ with high probability and the algorithm accepts.

Case (2): $\mathbf{v}_i = \mathbf{e}_{i1}\mathbf{f} + \mathbf{e}_{i2}\mathbf{g} \in \mathcal{D}_{\mathrm{ASSV}_{\mathbf{h},K}}$: Then $\mathbf{e}_{i1}\mathbf{f}, \mathbf{e}_{i2}\mathbf{g} \in \mathcal{BN}_{\sigma,K,\varepsilon}$ and consider the following

$$\begin{aligned}
\mathbf{v}_i\mathbf{hs} + \mathbf{e}_i &= \mathbf{g}(\mathbf{e}_{i1} + \mathbf{e}_{i2}\mathbf{h})\mathbf{s} + \mathbf{e}_i \\
&= \mathbf{g}(\mathbf{e}_{i1} + \mathbf{e}_{i2}\mathbf{h})(\mathbf{s} + \frac{\mathbf{v}_i}{\mathbf{e}_{i1} + \mathbf{e}_{i2}\mathbf{h}}) + \mathbf{e}_i - \mathbf{v}_i\mathbf{g} \\
&= \mathbf{g}(\mathbf{e}_{i1} + \mathbf{e}_{i2}\mathbf{h})(\mathbf{s} + \mathbf{f}) + \mathbf{e}_i - \mathbf{v}_i\mathbf{g}
\end{aligned}$$

As the standard deviation of the distribution used to sample the coordinates of $\mathbf{g}$ is σ_g, then $\mathbf{v}_i\mathbf{g}$ follows $\mathcal{N}_{\sigma_2}^n$, where $\sigma_2 = \sqrt{2n}\sigma\sigma_g$. Since $\sigma_e > \sigma_2$ and χ_{σ_e} is "wider" than the distribution of $\mathbf{v}_i\mathbf{g}$, then $(\mathbf{u}_i\mathbf{h}, \mathbf{u}_i\mathbf{hs} + \mathbf{e}_i)$ "information-theoretically hide" the value of $\mathbf{s}$. So, there are many possibilities for the secret and errors that are consistent with the pairs $(\mathbf{u}_i\mathbf{h}, \mathbf{u}_i\mathbf{hs} + \mathbf{e}_i)$, for example, $\mathbf{s} + \mathbf{f}$ and $\mathbf{e}_i - \mathbf{v}_i\mathbf{g}$. Therefore, no matter how the oracle $\mathcal{O}$ works internally, even the input pairs are not properly distributed RLWE samples. So, the oracle will reject it and the algorithm will also reject it. Hence, the search RLWE oracle could be used to solve the DASSV problem.

5   New Lattice-Based Signature

In this section, we construct a new provably secure signature scheme based on NTRU lattices. We recall the definition of a signature scheme that normally involves three algorithms, that is, key generation $\mathcal{K}$, signature generation $\mathcal{S}$ and signature verification $\mathcal{V}$. A formal definition is described as follows:

Definition 14. *A digital signature scheme $(\mathcal{K}, \mathcal{S}, \mathcal{V})$ consists of three algorithms, which are defined as follows:*

- *The key generation algorithm $\mathcal{K}$ takes a security parameter λ and returns a key pair (pk, sk), where pk is a public key and sk is a private key; we write $(pk, sk) \longleftarrow \mathcal{K}$.*
- *The signing algorithm $\mathcal{S}$ takes the private key sk and a message m and returns a signature σ; we write $\sigma \longleftarrow \mathcal{S}(sk, m)$*
- *The verification algorithm $\mathcal{V}$ takes the public key pk, a message-signature pair (m, σ) and returns either true or false; we write $\mathcal{V}(pk, m, \sigma) = true$ or false.*

Definition 15 (EUF-CMA Security). *A signature scheme is existential unforgeable under adaptive chosen message attack* (EUF-CMA) *if for any polynomial-time adversary* $\mathcal{A}$, *the probability of winning the following game is negligible.*

- **Set Up:** *The challenger* $\mathcal{C}$ *runs key generation algorithm* $\mathcal{K}$ *and produces a pair of public keys pk and secret key sk, and sends pk to the adversary* $\mathcal{A}$.
- **Signature Queries:** *The adversary* $\mathcal{A}$ *issues signature queries on messages* $m_1, \cdots, m_t$ *from the message space. The challenger* $\mathcal{C}$ *runs the signing algorithm* $\mathcal{S}$ *to generate signature* σ_i *for message* m_i *and sends these corresponding signatures* $\sigma_1, \cdots, \sigma_t$ *to the adversary* $\mathcal{A}$.
- **Output:** *Finally, the adversary* $\mathcal{A}$ *produces a pair of* (m', σ') *where* m' *is not from* $\{m_1, \cdots, m_t\}$ *and* σ' *is a valid signature.*

Define the success probability of an adversary $\mathcal{A}$ *as* $\Pr[\text{Succ}_{\mathcal{A}}^{\text{EUF-CMA}}(\lambda) = 1]$.

Our proposed lattice-based signature is based on NTRU lattices and Fiat-Shamir framework without aborts. The main idea of the proposed signature is to change the ephemeral secret key for each signature creation. This is to resist the statistical attack on fixed secret key.

Key Generation: Let n be a power of 2 and q be prime, $t, b_v, b_s, \hat{b}_v, \hat{b}_s$ be five integers such that $b_v \ll b_s$ and $\hat{b}_v \ll \hat{b}_s$. Let $t_1 = \lfloor \frac{n}{3} \rfloor$ and $\mathcal{H}$ be a hash function from $\{-1, 0, 1\}^* \times \mathcal{R}_q^3$ to $\{-1, 0, 1\}^n$. To generate a private and public key pairs, the sender performs the following:

(1) Choose two random secret polynomials $\mathbf{f}, \mathbf{g} \in \mathcal{F}_{t_1}$ such that $\mathbf{f}$ and $\mathbf{g}$ are unit elements in $\mathcal{R}_q$.
(2) Compute $\mathbf{h} = \mathbf{f}^{-1}\mathbf{g} \in \mathcal{R}_q^*$.
(3) Then, the public key is $\mathbf{h}$ and the secret key is $(\mathbf{f}, \mathbf{g})$.

Signing: Let $\mathbf{m}$ be a message to be signed. The signing process is as follows:

(1) Choose $\mathbf{e}_1, \mathbf{e}_2 \in \mathcal{E}_t$, $\mathbf{u}_1, \mathbf{u}_2 \in \mathcal{U}_{b_s/2}$, compute

$$\mathbf{v} = \mathbf{e}_1\mathbf{f} + \mathbf{e}_2\mathbf{g}, \qquad \mathbf{w} = \mathbf{u}_1\mathbf{h}^{-1} + \mathbf{u}_2\mathbf{h}, \qquad \mathbf{c} = \mathcal{H}(\mathbf{m}, \mathbf{v}, \mathbf{w}, \mathbf{h}) \in \mathcal{E}_{t_2},$$
$$\mathbf{s}_1 = \mathbf{u}_1 + \mathbf{c}\mathbf{e}_1\mathbf{g}, \qquad \mathbf{s}_2 = \mathbf{u}_2 + \mathbf{c}\mathbf{e}_2\mathbf{f}.$$

(2) Then, the signature is $(\mathbf{v}, \mathbf{c}, \mathbf{s}_1, \mathbf{s}_2)$.

We note that $\mathbf{v} \in \mathcal{D}_{b_v}$ and $\mathbf{s}_1, \mathbf{s}_2 \in \mathcal{D}_{b_s}$ with high probability due to our choice of parameters explained in Sect. 7.1. This means that each signature will not be rejected for each signature generation with very high probability. This is different from those signature schemes based on Fiat-Shamir with aborts, which require to reject a number of signatures before the correct signature generated.

Verification: Verify the signature $(\mathbf{v}, \mathbf{c}, \mathbf{s}_1, \mathbf{s}_2)$ as follows:

(1) Compute $\mathbf{w}' = \mathbf{s}_1\mathbf{h}^{-1} + \mathbf{s}_2\mathbf{h} - \mathbf{c}\mathbf{v} = \mathbf{u}_1\mathbf{h}^{-1} + \mathbf{u}_2\mathbf{h}$.

(2) Check the following

$$\mathbf{c} \stackrel{?}{=} \mathcal{H}(\mathbf{m}, \mathbf{v}, \mathbf{w}', \mathbf{h}), \ \|\mathbf{v}\|_\infty \stackrel{?}{\leq} b_v, \ \|\mathbf{s}_i\|_\infty \stackrel{?}{\leq} b_s, \ \|\mathbf{v}\| \stackrel{?}{\leq} \hat{b}_v, \ \|\mathbf{s}_i\| \stackrel{?}{\leq} \hat{b}_s \text{ for } i = 1, 2.$$

(3) If all the above checks are correct, then accept the signature, otherwise, reject.

The signing process needs 4 polynomials additions and 8 polynomials multiplications in $\mathcal{R}_q$. On the other hand, the verification process needs 2 polynomials additions/subtractions and 3 polynomials multiplications in $\mathcal{R}_q$. Hence, the computation of both signing and verification are efficient.

6 Security Proof and Analysis of the Proposed Signature

In this section, we will give a security proof and key recovery analysis of the proposed signature in Sect. 6.1 and Sect. 6.2 respectively.

6.1 Security Proof of the Proposed Signature

In this section, we will give the security proof of the proposed signature and show that it is secure in the random oracle model based on the following assumptions.

Assumption 4 (SmVecP$_{\hat{\mathbf{h}},K}$ Assumption). *The Small Vectors assumption is the assumption that the advantage* $\mathrm{Adv}_{\mathrm{SmVP}_{\hat{\mathbf{h}},K}}(\mathcal{A})$ *is negligible, i.e.,* $\mathrm{Adv}_{\mathrm{SmVP}_{\hat{\mathbf{h}},K}}(\mathcal{A}) \leq \varepsilon_{\mathrm{SmVP}_{\hat{\mathbf{h}},K}}$.

Assumption 5 (DASSV$_{\mathbf{h},K}$ Assumption). *The Decision Advance Sum of Small Vector assumption is the assumption that the advantage* $\mathrm{Adv}_{\mathrm{DASSV}_{\mathbf{h},K}}(\mathcal{A})$ *is negligible, i.e.,* $\mathrm{Adv}_{\mathrm{DASSV}_{\mathbf{h},K}}(\mathcal{A}) \leq \varepsilon_{\mathrm{DASSV}_{\mathbf{h},K}}$.

Assumption 6 (DSSV$_{\mathbf{h},K}$ Assumption). *The Decision Sum of Small Vector assumption is the assumption that the advantage* $\mathrm{Adv}_{\mathrm{DSSV}_{\mathbf{h},K}}(\mathcal{A})$ *is negligible, i.e.,* $\mathrm{Adv}_{\mathrm{DSSV}_{\mathbf{h},K}}(\mathcal{A}) \leq \varepsilon_{\mathrm{DSSV}_{\mathbf{h},K}}$.

It is noted that we may substitute $\mathbf{h}$ with $\mathbf{h}^{-1}$ in Assumption 6 to obtain the DSSV$_{\mathbf{h}^{-1},K}$ assumption.

Theorem 2. *Under the* DASSV$_{\mathbf{h},K}$, DSSV$_{\mathbf{h},K}$, DSSV$_{\mathbf{h}^{-1},K}$ *and* SmVecP$_{\hat{\mathbf{h}},K}$ *assumptions and the hardness of* DNTRU *problem, then the proposed signature scheme is existentially unforgeable under adaptive chosen-message attacks (EUF-CMA) in the random oracle model.*

Proof. Let $\mathcal{LS}$ be the proposed signature scheme, and let $\mathcal{A}$ be a PPT (probabilistic polynomial time) adversary attacking $\mathcal{LS}$. In order to analyse the success probability of the adversary $\mathcal{A}$, we proceed by introducing a sequence of games $\mathbf{G}_0, \cdots, \mathbf{G}_3$. Let $\mathrm{Pr}[\mathbf{G}_i]$ denote the probability that the game $\mathbf{G}_i$ returns 1 at the end of game $\mathbf{G}_i$. The sequence of games are described as follows:

- **Game G_0:** This is the standard game of EUF-CMA for the signature scheme $\mathcal{LS}$. The adversary $\mathcal{A}$ can access to the signing oracle to obtain valid signatures. Then,

$$\Pr[G_0] = \Pr[\text{Succ}_{\mathcal{A}}^{\text{EUF-CMA}}(\lambda) = 1].$$

- **Game G_1:** In Game G_0, we have $\mathbf{v} = \mathbf{e_1 f} + \mathbf{e_2 g}$, now we replace $\mathbf{v}$ by a random vector $\mathbf{v}' \in \mathcal{D}_{b_v}$. The adversary $\mathcal{A}$ will not notice this change as the change is a $\text{DASSV}_{\mathbf{h},K}$ problem which is indistinguishable. Therefore, we have

$$\big| \Pr[G_1] - \Pr[G_0] \big| \leq \varepsilon_{\text{DASSV}_{\mathbf{h},K}}.$$

In this setting, compute $\mathbf{w}' = \mathbf{s_1 h}^{-1} + \mathbf{s_2 h} - \mathbf{c}'\mathbf{v}'$. Then query random oracle $\mathcal{O}_H$ on $\mathbf{w}', \mathbf{v}', \mathbf{h}$ and set $\mathbf{c}' = \mathcal{H}(\mathbf{m}, \mathbf{v}', \mathbf{w}', \mathbf{h})$.

- **Game G_2:** In this game, we replace $\mathbf{s_1}, \mathbf{s_2}$ by random $\mathbf{s_1}', \mathbf{s_2}' \in \mathcal{D}_{b_s}$. As these changes are $\text{DSSV}_{\mathbf{h}^{-1},K}$ problem and $\text{DSSV}_{\mathbf{h},K}$ problem respectively which are indistinguishable, so the adversary $\mathcal{A}$ will not notice these changes. Therefore, we have

$$\big| \Pr[G_2] - \Pr[G_1] \big| \leq \varepsilon_{\text{DSSV}_{\mathbf{h},K}} + \varepsilon_{\text{DSSV}_{\mathbf{h}^{-1},K}}.$$

In this setting, compute $\mathbf{w}'' = \mathbf{s_1}'\mathbf{h}^{-1} + \mathbf{s_2}'\mathbf{h} - \mathbf{c}''\mathbf{v}'$. Then query random oracle $\mathcal{O}_H$ on $\mathbf{w}'', \mathbf{v}', \mathbf{h}$ and output $\mathbf{c}'' = \mathcal{H}(\mathbf{m}, \mathbf{v}', \mathbf{w}'', \mathbf{h})$.

- **Game G_3:** We now replace $\mathbf{h} = \mathbf{f}^{-1}\mathbf{g}$ by a random vector $\hat{\mathbf{h}} \in \mathcal{R}_q^*$. This change corresponds to an instance of the DNTRU problem. So, the adversary $\mathcal{A}$ will not notice the change as DNTRU problem is indistinguishable. Therefore, we have $\big| \Pr[G_3] - \Pr[G_2] \big| \leq \varepsilon_{\text{DNTRU}}$.

At this step, the public key is random and independent from the secret key. Hence, the security of the scheme is reduced to the case where no signature is given to the adversary. The adversary $\mathcal{A}$ only has information of public key as $\hat{\mathbf{h}}$. If the adversary $\mathcal{A}$ can compute a valid signature $(\bar{\mathbf{v}}, \bar{\mathbf{c}}, \bar{\mathbf{s}}_1, \bar{\mathbf{s}}_2)$ in **Game G_3**, then the adversary $\mathcal{A}$ can compute $\bar{\mathbf{v}}$, that is, the adversary $\mathcal{A}$ must solve the small vector problem $(\text{SmVP}_{\hat{\mathbf{h}},K})$ with the advantage less than $\varepsilon_{\text{SmVP}_{\hat{\mathbf{h}},K}}$. Therefore, we have

$$\Pr[G_3] \leq \varepsilon_{\text{SmVP}_{\hat{\mathbf{h}},K}}.$$

From **Game G_0** to **Game G_3**, we have

$$\big| \Pr[G_0] - \Pr[G_3] \big| = \left| \sum_{i=0}^{2} \big(\Pr[G_i] - \Pr[G_{i+1}] \big) \right|$$

$$\leq \sum_{i=0}^{2} \big| \Pr[G_i] - \Pr[G_{i+1}] \big|$$

$$= \sum_{i=0}^{2} \big| \Pr[G_{i+1}] - \Pr[G_i] \big|.$$

Hence,

$$\Pr[\mathbf{G}_0] \leq \sum_{i=0}^{2} \big| \Pr[\mathbf{G}_{i+1}] - \Pr[\mathbf{G}_i] \big| + \Pr[\mathbf{G}_3]$$

$$\leq \varepsilon_{\mathrm{DASSV}_{\mathbf{h},K}} + \varepsilon_{\mathrm{DSSV}_{\mathbf{h},K}} + \varepsilon_{\mathrm{DSSV}_{\mathbf{h}-1,K}} + \varepsilon_{\mathrm{DNTRU}} + \varepsilon_{\mathrm{SmVP}_{\mathbf{fi},K}}.$$

6.2 Analysis of Key Recovery Attacks

Given a public key $\mathbf{h} = \mathbf{f}^{-1}\mathbf{g}$, the adversary is to find $\mathbf{f}, \mathbf{g}$. There are four approaches to do this, namely, exhaustive search of $\mathbf{f}$, lattice attack to find shortest vector of a lattice, subfield attack on a lattice, and hybrid attack.

(1) **Key Exhaustive Search:** For NTRU with ternary secret key over $\{-1, 0, 1\}^n$ with means $\frac{1}{n}$, let -1 appears t_1 times and 1 appears $t_1 + 1$ times, zero appears $n - 2t_1 - 1$, where $t_1 = \lfloor \frac{n}{3} \rfloor$, then the total number of searching $\mathbf{f}$ is at least $\frac{1}{n} C_{t_1}^n C_{t_1+1}^{n-t_1}$ (The factor $1/n$ comes from the fact that an attacker can guess any of the n cyclic rotations of the secret key, rather than just the secret key itself). For example, if $n = 1024$, then we have at least 2^{1602} possible keys. By key search of ternary LWE [20], the complexity of key search is at least $(2^{1602})^{0.24} \approx 2^{384.48}$ (classical) and $(2^{1602})^{0.19} \approx 2^{304.38}$ (quantum) respectively. Hence, the exhaustive search attack has exponential time complexity.

(2) **Lattice Attack:** To find $\mathbf{f}, \mathbf{g}$ in $\mathbf{h} = (h_0, \cdots, h_{n-1})$, one could find a shortest vector of the lattice $L = \begin{bmatrix} \mathbf{I}_n & \mathbf{h} \\ \mathbf{0}_n & q\mathbf{I}_n \end{bmatrix}$ via BKZ algorithm. Then $(\mathbf{f}, \mathbf{e})L = (\mathbf{f}, \mathbf{g})$ as $f(x)h(x) = g(x) - qe(x)(x^n + 1)$ in $\mathcal{R}_q$ for some $e(x) \in \mathcal{R}_q$. So, $(\mathbf{f}, \mathbf{g})$ is a short vector of the lattice $\mathcal{L}$.

The best known algorithm to find the shortest vector is BKZ 2.0 algorithm [10], with time complexity $2^{0.292\beta+o(\beta)}$ and $2^{0.265\beta+o(\beta)}$ in classical and quantum computer respectively [5], where β is the block size. It is believed that the current technique of BKZ 2.0 algorithm [10] is only able to find a shortest vector with a root Hermite factor of at least 1.005. If β is large, then BKZ algorithm has exponential time complexity. Hence, finding $\mathbf{f}, \mathbf{g}$ from the public key $\mathbf{h}$ via BKZ algorithm has exponential time complexity.

(3) **Subfield Attack:** One of the powerful attack on NTRU lattices is called subfield attack, which has been considered in [7]. In [2,24] and [29], they exploit the subfield attack for certain "over-stretched" NTRU parameters with ring $\mathbb{Z}_q[x]/(x^n + 1)$, where n is a power of 2. But this attack only applies to the NTRU lattices with large q that are used to instantiate a (fully) homomorphic encryption. Recently, Ducas and Woerden [14] gave a fatigue point for q to be $0.004n^{2.484}$. This means that subfield attack will not be applicable for $q < 0.004n^{2.484}$. Based on this fatigue point, our parameters (refer to Sect. 7.2) for q and n are chosen such that $q < 0.004n^{2.484}$ (e.g. $q = 18433, n = 1024$ and $0.004n^{2.484} = 120128.23 > q$). Hence, our scheme is not subject to the subfield attacks.

(4) **Hybrid Attack:** The hybrid attack [21] is a hybrid of lattice attack and meet-in-the-middle attack. The hybrid attack was first proposed to perform attack on NTRU and it was later revised [35] to attack special lattices which have similar structure to NTRU as $L = \begin{bmatrix} \mathbf{I}_n & \mathbf{h} \\ \mathbf{0}_n & q\mathbf{I}_n \end{bmatrix}$ and $L' = \begin{bmatrix} \mathbf{C} & \mathbf{A} \\ \mathbf{0} & \mathbf{B} \end{bmatrix}$, where $(\mathbf{f}, \mathbf{e})L = (\mathbf{f}, \mathbf{g})$ and $(\mathbf{v_f}, \mathbf{v_e})L' = (\mathbf{v_f}, \mathbf{v_g})$. The idea of hybrid attack is to reduce the dimension of the original lattice and preserve the determinant of the original lattice by guessing a small number of coordinates of the unknown $\mathbf{f}$ or $\mathbf{v}_f$ (i.e. the first few coordinates of $\mathbf{f}$ and $\mathbf{v}_f$ respectively). According to [35], the complexity of hybrid attacks on NTRU [19] and NTRU prime [8] are higher than the claimed security level. Our lattice is similar to NTRU prime. Applying the analysis of the hybrid attack in [35], the hybrid attack will not be a threat to our signature scheme as our security parameters are chosen to be secure against this attack.

7   Suggested Parameters

7.1   Parameters of $b_v, b_s, \hat{b}_v, \hat{b}_s$

We choose $b_v = k\sigma_\mathbf{v}$ and $b_s = 2k\sigma_\mathbf{s}$, where $\sigma_\mathbf{v}$ and $\sigma_\mathbf{s}$ are the standard deviations of the coordinates of $\mathbf{v}$ and $\mathbf{ce_1g}$ (and $\mathbf{ce_2f}$) respectively, such that $\mathbf{v} \in \mathcal{D}_{b_v}$ and $\mathbf{s}_1, \mathbf{s}_2 \in \mathcal{D}_{b_s}$ with high probability. By Proposition 1, the probability is at least $1 - \min\{1, \frac{n}{2}(e^{-k^2} + e^{-k^2/2})\}$. So, choosing $k = 10$, the probability is at least $1 - 2^{-62}$.

Since $\mathbf{f}, \mathbf{g}$ follows the distribution $\mathcal{F}_{t_1}$ with mean $\frac{1}{n}$ and variance $\frac{2t_1 n + n - 1}{n^2}$ and $\mathbf{e}_1, \mathbf{e}_2$ follows the distribution $\mathcal{E}_t$ with mean 0 and variance $\frac{t}{n}$, then by Corollary 1 and Lemma 5 (1) , each coordinate of $\mathbf{e_1 f}$ and $\mathbf{e_2 g}$ approximates to $\mathcal{N}\left(0, \frac{t(2t_1+1)}{n}\right)$. Thus, each coordinate of $\mathbf{v} = \mathbf{e_1 f} + \mathbf{e_2 g}$ approximates to $\mathcal{N}(0, \sigma_\mathbf{v}^2)$, where $\sigma_\mathbf{v} = \sqrt{\frac{2t(2t_1+1)}{n}}$. We take $b_v = 10\sigma_\mathbf{v} = 10\sqrt{\frac{2t(2t_1+1)}{n}}$ and $\hat{b}_v = 1.1\sigma_\mathbf{v}\sqrt{n}$.

Similar to the above argument, each coordinate of $\mathbf{e_1 g}$ approximates to $\mathcal{N}(0, \sigma_1^2)$, where $\sigma_1 = \sqrt{\frac{t(2t_1+1)}{n}}$ and $\mathbf{c}$ is also taken from $\mathcal{E}_{t_2}$, where $t_2 \geq t$. Recall that $\mathcal{E}_{t_2}$ is a distribution with mean 0 and variance $\frac{t_2}{n}$. By Lemma 5 (2), each coordinate of $\mathbf{ce_1 g}$ approximates to $\mathcal{N}(0, \sigma_2^2)$, where $\sigma_2^2 = \frac{t(2t_1+1)}{n} * \frac{t_2}{n} * n = \frac{t t_2(2t_1+1)}{n}$. We let $b_{s_1} = 10\sigma_2 = 10\sqrt{\frac{t t_2(2t_1+1)}{n}}$. Since $\mathbf{s}_1 = \mathbf{u}_1 + \mathbf{ce_1 g}$, let $\mathbf{u}_1 \in \mathcal{D}_{b_{s_1}}$. As $\mathbf{s}_2$ is similar to $\mathbf{s}_1$, so, we let $b_s = 2b_{s_1} = 20\sqrt{\frac{t t_2(2t_1+1)}{n}}$ and $\hat{b}_s = \sqrt{(\frac{2b_{s_1}(b_{s_1}+1)}{3} + \sigma_2^2)n}$.

With $b_v = 10\sqrt{\frac{2t(2t_1+1)}{n}}$ and $b_s = 20\sqrt{\frac{t t_2(2t_1+1)}{n}}$, then the probability of $\mathbf{v} \in \mathcal{D}_{b_v}$, $\mathbf{s}_1 \in \mathcal{D}_{b_s}$ and $\mathbf{s}_2 \in \mathcal{D}_{b_s}$ are at least $1 - \min\{1, \frac{n}{2}(e^{-k^2} + e^{-k^2/2})\}$ respectively. Then, we obtain the following table (Table 1).

Table 1. Parameters for $t, t_1, b_v, b_s, \hat{b}_v, \hat{b}_s$

n	t	$t_1 = \lfloor \frac{n}{3} \rfloor$	t_2	b_v	b_s	$\hat{b}_v$	$\hat{b}_s$	Approx. Prob.
512	44	170	44	76	718	189	6691	$> 1 - 2^{-64}$
1024	60	341	60	89	980	313	12911	$> 1 - 2^{-63}$
2048	120	682	120	126	1958	627	36463	$> 1 - 2^{-62}$

7.2 Security Parameters

The most successful approach to solve $\mathbf{h}$ in NTRU is by converting this problem into solving the shortest vector problem (SVP) in lattice and then applying lattice reduction algorithm that solves this [3]. The best algorithm for finding shortest vector problem in practice is the Block-Korkine-Zolotarev (BKZ) algorithm [10].

Given $\mathbf{h} = \mathbf{f}^{-1}\mathbf{g} \bmod q$ in NTRU, we construct a lattice $\bar{\mathcal{L}}$ of dimension $2n$ as $\begin{bmatrix} \mathbf{I}_n & \mathbf{h} \\ \mathbf{0}_n & q\mathbf{I}_n \end{bmatrix}$. The lattice $\bar{\mathcal{L}}$ has an SVP solution $\mathbf{v} = (\mathbf{f}, \mathbf{g})$. The time complexity for finding shortest vector in BKZ algorithm with block size β is $2^{0.292n+o(\beta)}$ and $2^{0.265n+o(\beta)}$ in classical and quantum computer respectively [5]. Based on the appropriate block size β of BKZ algorithm for n and q, we compute the public key size, secret key size and signature size as $n * (\lfloor \log_2 q \rfloor + 1)/8$ bytes, $4n/8$ bytes and $n * (2 + \lceil \log_2 b_v \rceil + 1 + 2(\lceil \log_2 b_s \rceil + 1))/8$ bytes respectively. Then, we list the public key, secret key and signature key at different security level in the following Table 2.

Table 2. Parameters at different security level

PQ security level	n	q	$PK_{Size[bytes]}$	$SK_{Size[bytes]}$	$SIG_{Size[bytes]}$
80	512	12289	896	256	2048
180	1024	18433	1920	512	4096
264	2048	40961	4096	1024	8704

In the above security parameters of the proposed signature scheme, we compare with those publicly known lattice-based signature schemes in the following Table 3.

Table 3. Comparisons with other signature schemes

Scheme	PQ security	n	q	PK_{Size} [bytes]	SK_{Size}[bytes]	SIG_{Size}[bytes]
Dilithium [13]	128	256(5x4)	8380417	1472	3504	2701
Falcon [18]	103	512	12289	896	7553	666
qTESLA [4]	139	1024	43576577	14880	5224	2592
MLS [12]	149	1024	$2^{16}+1$	2048	103	2048
BCM [6]	170 (classical)	512(3x5)	$\approx 2^{31}$	9952	5952	6021
MITAKA [16]	92	512	12889	896	16000	713
This paper	180	1024	18433	1920	512	4096

As it can be seen in Table 3, the public key size of the proposed signature scheme is smaller than all of the above signature schemes except for Falcon, Dilithium and MITAKA. But Falcon, Dilithium and MITAKA are 103-bit, 128-bit and 92-bit quantum security respectively, while the proposed signature scheme achieves 180-bit quantum security. The secret key size of the proposed signature scheme is smaller than all other signature schemes except for the MLS schemes. Although the signature size of the proposed signature scheme is slightly larger than all of the above schemes (except BCM), but the proposed signature scheme achieves higher security. It is noted that BCM is of 170-bit classical security.

8   Conclusion

In this paper, we defined a number of new hard problems on NTRU lattices and showed that the search RLWE problem is as hard as these new hard problems. Then, we constructed a new lattice-based signature scheme which is based on NTRU lattices and Fiat-Shamir framework without aborts in order to avoid the side channel attacks exploiting the weakness in the "Fiat-Shamir with aborts" framework. The proposed signature scheme is based on the trapdoor of NTRU lattices, that is, $\mathbf{h} = \mathbf{f}^{-1}\mathbf{g}$ such that $\mathbf{f}, \mathbf{g}$ are short vectors. Then, we gave a security proof of the proposed signature against existential forgery under the chosen message attacks in the random oracle model. The security proof is based on those new problems. The public key size, secret key size and signature size of the proposed signature scheme are 1920 bytes, 512 bytes and 4096 bytes respectively for 180-bit quantum security level. The key and signature sizes of the proposed signature scheme is comparable to those of the currently known signatures, such as, Dilithium [13], Falcon [18], qTESLA [4], MLS [12], BCM [6] and MITAKA [16].

References

1. Ajtai, M.: The shortest vector problem in L2 is NP-hard for randomized reductions (extended abstract). In: 30th Annual ACM Symposium on Theory of Computing Proceedings, pp. 10–19 (1998). https://doi.org/10.1145/276698.276705
2. Albrecht, M., Bai, S., Ducas, L.: A subfield lattice attack on overstretched NTRU assumptions. In: Robshaw, M., Katz, J. (eds.) CRYPTO 2016, Part I. LNCS, vol. 9814, pp. 153–178. Springer, Heidelberg (2016). https://doi.org/10.1007/978-3-662-53018-4_6
3. Albrecht, M.R., Göpfert, F., Virdia, F., Wunderer, T.: Revisiting the expected cost of solving uSVP and applications to LWE. In: Takagi, T., Peyrin, T. (eds.) ASIACRYPT 2017, Part I. LNCS, vol. 10624, pp. 297–322. Springer, Cham (2017). https://doi.org/10.1007/978-3-319-70694-8_11
4. Alkim, E., Barreto, P.S.L.M., Bindel, N., Krämer, J., Longa, P., Ricardini, J.E.: The lattice-based digital signature scheme qTESLA. In: Conti, M., Zhou, J., Casalicchio, E., Spognardi, A. (eds.) ACNS 2020. LNCS, vol. 12146, pp. 441–460. Springer, Cham (2020). https://doi.org/10.1007/978-3-030-57808-4_22
5. Bai, S., Laarhoven, T., Stehlé, D.: Tuple lattice sieving. LMS J. Comput. Math. **19**, 146–162 (2016). https://doi.org/10.1112/S1461157016000292
6. Behnia, R., Chen, Y., Masny, D.: On removing rejection conditions in practical lattice-based signatures. In: Cheon, J.H., Tillich, J.-P. (eds.) PQCrypto 2021 2021. LNCS, vol. 12841, pp. 380–398. Springer, Cham (2021). https://doi.org/10.1007/978-3-030-81293-5_20
7. Bernstein, D.J.: A subfield-logarithm attack against ideal lattices. The cr.yp.to blog. https://blog.cr.yp.to/20140213-ideal.html. Accessed 3 May 2021
8. Bernstein, D.J., Chuengsatiansup, C., Lange, T., van Vredendaal, C.: NTRU prime: reducing attack surface at low cost. In: Adams, C., Camenisch, J. (eds.) SAC 2017. LNCS, vol. 10719, pp. 235–260. Springer, Cham (2018). https://doi.org/10.1007/978-3-319-72565-9_12
9. Groot Bruinderink, L., Pessl, P.: Differential fault attacks on deterministic lattice signatures. In: IACR TCHES 2018, pp. 21–43 (2018). https://tches.iacr.org/index.php/TCHES/article/view/7267
10. Chen, Y., Nguyen, P.Q.: BKZ 2.0: better lattice security estimates. In: Lee, D.H., Wang, X. (eds.) ASIACRYPT 2011. LNCS, vol. 7073, pp. 1–20. Springer, Heidelberg (2011). https://doi.org/10.1007/978-3-642-25385-0_1
11. Chiani, M., Dardari, D., Simon, M.K.: New exponential bounds and approximations for the computation of error probability in fading channels. IEEE Trans. Wireless Commun. **2**(4), 840–845 (2003)
12. Das, D., Hoffstein, J., Pipher, J., Whyte, W., Zhang, Z.: Modular lattice signatures, revisited. Des. Codes Crypt. **88**(3), 505–532 (2019). https://doi.org/10.1007/s10623-019-00694-x
13. Ducas, L., et al.: Crystals-dilithium: a lattice-based digital signature scheme. IACR Trans. Cryptogr. Hardw. Embed. Syst. **2018**(1), 238–268 (2018). https://doi.org/10.13154/tches.v2018.i1.238-268
14. Ducas, L., van Woerden, W.: NTRU fatigue: how stretched is overstretched? In: Tibouchi, M., Wang, H. (eds.) ASIACRYPT 2021. LNCS, vol. 13093, pp. 3–32. Springer, Cham (2021). https://doi.org/10.1007/978-3-030-92068-5_1
15. Espitau, T., Fouque, P., Gérard, B., Tibouchi, M.: Loop-abort faults on lattice-based signature schemes and key exchange protocols. IEEE Trans. Comput. **67**(11), 1535–1549 (2018). https://doi.org/10.1109/TC.2018.2833119

16. Espitau, T., et al.: MITAKA: a simpler, parallelizable, maskable variant of FAL-CON. In: Dunkelman, O., Dziembowski, S. (eds.) EUROCRYPT 2022. LNCS, vol. 13277, pp. 222–253. Springer, Cham (2022). https://doi.org/10.1007/978-3-031-07082-2_9

17. Fiat, A., Shamir, A.: How to prove yourself: practical solutions to identification and signature problems. In: Odlyzko, A.M. (ed.) CRYPTO 1986. LNCS, vol. 263, pp. 186–194. Springer, Heidelberg (1987). https://doi.org/10.1007/3-540-47721-7_12

18. Fouque, P.-A., et al.: FALCON: fast-Fourier lattice-based compact signatures over NTRU (2020). https://falcon-sign.info/falcon.pdf

19. Hoffstein, J., Pipher, J., Silverman, J.H.: NTRU: a ring-based public key cryptosystem. In: Buhler, J.P. (ed.) ANTS 1998. LNCS, vol. 1423, pp. 267–288. Springer, Heidelberg (1998). https://doi.org/10.1007/BFb0054868

20. van Hoof, I., Kirshanova, E., May, A.: Quantum key search for ternary LWE. In: Cheon, J.H., Tillich, J.-P. (eds.) PQCrypto 2021 2021. LNCS, vol. 12841, pp. 117–132. Springer, Cham (2021). https://doi.org/10.1007/978-3-030-81293-5_7

21. Howgrave-Graham, N.: A hybrid lattice-reduction and meet-in-the-middle attack against NTRU. In: Menezes, A. (ed.) CRYPTO 2007. LNCS, vol. 4622, pp. 150–169. Springer, Heidelberg (2007). https://doi.org/10.1007/978-3-540-74143-5_9

22. Karabulut, E., Aysu, A.: FALCON down: breaking FALCON post-quantum signature scheme through side-channel attacks. In: 58th ACM/IEEE Design Automation Conference (DAC), pp. 691–696. IEEE (2021). https://doi.org/10.1109/DAC18074.2021.9586131

23. Kim, I.J., Lee, T.H., Han, J., Sim, B.Y., Han, D.G.: Novel single-trace ML profiling attacks on NIST 3 round candidate Dilithium. IACR Cryptology ePrint Archive 2020/1383 (2020). https://eprint.iacr.org/2020/1383

24. Kirchner, P., Fouque, P.-A.: Revisiting lattice attacks on overstretched NTRU parameters. In: Coron, J.-S., Nielsen, J.B. (eds.) EUROCRYPT 2017. LNCS, vol. 10210, pp. 3–26. Springer, Cham (2017). https://doi.org/10.1007/978-3-319-56620-7_1

25. Lenstra, A.K., Lenstra, H.W., Jr., Lovász, L.: Factoring polynomials with rational coefficients. Math. Ann. **261**(4), 515–534 (1982)

26. Lyubashevsky, V.: Fiat-Shamir with aborts: applications to lattice and factoring-based signatures. In: Matsui, M. (ed.) ASIACRYPT 2009. LNCS, vol. 5912, pp. 598–616. Springer, Heidelberg (2009). https://doi.org/10.1007/978-3-642-10366-7_35

27. Lyubashevsky, V.: Lattice signatures without trapdoors. In: Pointcheval, D., Johansson, T. (eds.) EUROCRYPT 2012. LNCS, vol. 7237, pp. 738–755. Springer, Heidelberg (2012). https://doi.org/10.1007/978-3-642-29011-4_43

28. Lyubashevsky, V., Peikert, C., Regev, O.: A toolkit for ring-LWE cryptography. In: Johansson, T., Nguyen, P.Q. (eds.) EUROCRYPT 2013. LNCS, vol. 7881, pp. 35–54. Springer, Heidelberg (2013). https://doi.org/10.1007/978-3-642-38348-9_3

29. Micheli, G.D., Heninger, N., Shani, B.: Characterizing overstretched NTRU attacks. J. Math. Cryptol. **14**(1), 110–119 (2020). https://doi.org/10.1515/jmc-2015-0055

30. Panaretos, V.M.: Statistics for Mathematicians – A Rigorous First Course. Brickhäuser Basel (2016). https://doi.org/10.1007/978-3-319-28341-8

31. Peikert, C.: A decade of lattice cryptography. Found. Trends Theoret. Comput. Sci. **10**(4), 283–424 (2016). https://doi.org/10.1561/0400000074

32. Pellet-Mary, A., Stehlé, D.: On the hardness of the NTRU problem. In: Tibouchi, M., Wang, H. (eds.) ASIACRYPT 2021. LNCS, vol. 13090, pp. 3–35. Springer, Cham (2021). https://doi.org/10.1007/978-3-030-92062-3_1

33. Ravi, P., Jhanwar, M.P., Howe, J., Chattopadhyay, A., Bhasin, S.: Exploiting determinism in lattice-based signatures: practical fault attacks on pqm4 implementations of NIST candidates. In: Asia CCS 2019, pp. 427–440. Association for Computing Machinery (2019). https://doi.org/10.1145/3321705.3329821
34. Schnorr, C.-P., Euchner, M.: Lattice basis reduction: improved practical algorithms and solving subset sum problems. Math. Program. **66**(1–3), 181–199 (1994). https://doi.org/10.1007/BF01581144
35. Wunderer, T.: A detailed analysis of the hybrid lattice-reduction and meet-in-the-middle attack. J. Math. Cryptol. **13**(1), 1–26 (2019). https://doi.org/10.1515/jmc-2016-0044

A Complementary Result on the Construction of Quadratic Cyclotomic Classes

Kamil Otal[1] and Eda Tekin[2(✉)]

[1] TÜBİTAK BİLGEM UEKAE, Gebze, Kocaeli, Turkey
kamil.otal@gmail.com
[2] Karabük University, Karabük, Turkey
tedatekin@gmail.com

Abstract. Side-channel analysis (SCA) is a general name for cryptanalytic methods based on side information gathered by measuring and analyzing of various physical parameters. Threshold implementation (TI) is one of the successful countermeasure techniques for some types of SCA. Within this scope, Nikova et al. gave an algorithm on the decomposition of power permutations into quadratic power permutations over finite fields $\mathbb{F}_{2^n}$ in [Cryptogr. Commun. 11, 37–384 (2019)]. Later on, Otal and Tekin gave a sufficient way in [Cryptogr. Commun. 13, 837–845 (2021)] to reduce the precomputation cost in the algorithm of Nikova et al. substantially. In this paper, we prove that this sufficient way is also necessary, in other words, the proposed way is an optimal solution. In that way, we provide a complementary result on the construction of quadratic cyclotomic classes.

Keywords: Boolean functions · S-boxes · Power permutations

1 Introduction

Classical cryptanalysis considers attack scenarios of possible adversaries in a cryptosystem. An adversary may have additional side-channel information by measuring or analyzing various physical parameters and thus be more powerful in real life. Side-channel analysis (SCA) aims to obtain some secret data using this extra information.

SCA and contermeasures to SCA have become of interest intensely especially in the last decade. SCA uses different methods such as monitoring the electromagnetic emanations, the acoustic produced by devices or the power consumption to obtain extra information. Simple, differential, and correlation power analysis are the most notable side-channel attacks (see [11] as a compact source to follow the advances in the field).

Threshold implementation (TI) is a masking technique proposed as a countermeasure to some types of SCA. In particular, TI provides secure countermeasures

A. Nitaj and K. Zkik (Eds.): I4CS 2022, CCIS 1747, pp. 77–82, 2022.
https://doi.org/10.1007/978-3-031-23201-5_5

against differential power analysis attacks. For implementation purposes, decomposition of S-boxes into smaller (even quadratic) maps is an important question [7]. Decomposition of power permutations and their cycle structure has been studied and some decomposition techniques of permutations for side-channel attacks have been given in [2,4,5,9].

1.1   Related Work

Nikova et al. gave an algorithm on decomposition of power permutations into quadratic power permutations over finite fields $\mathbb{F}_{2^n}$ in [9]. To obtain quadratic permutations, they first apply a precomputation to find all cyclotomic classes of $\mathbb{F}_{2^n}$, then they use the quadratic ones among these classes.

Later, Otal and Tekin gave an efficient way in [10] to reduce the precomputation cost in the algorithm of Nikova et al. drastically. In particular, they proposed a small set which consists of <u>at least</u> one element from each cyclotomic class.

1.2   Our Contribution

In this paper we examine whether the small set given in [10] can be reduced further. That is, we try to understand whether the set consists of <u>at most</u> one element from each cyclotomic class. As a result, we prove that the answer is affirmative and hence show that the solution proposed in [10] is an optimal solution.

1.3   Organization of the Paper

The paper is organised as follows. In Sect. 2 we give some preliminary information and restate the algorithm in [9]. We present our main result, Theorem 2, and prove it in Sect. 3. In the last section, we conclude the paper summarizing our contribution.

2   Preliminaries

In this section, we first give some fundamental notions and then state the algorithm in [9] for the sake of completeness.

Let $n > 2$ be an integer, $\mathbb{F}_{2^n}$ denote the finite field of size 2^n, and $f : \mathbb{F}_{2^n} \to \mathbb{F}_{2^n}$ be a permutation polynomial. A finite sequence of t permutation polynomials $f_1, \ldots, f_t$ over $\mathbb{F}_{2^n}$ satisfying

$$f = f_t \circ \cdots \circ f_1$$

is called a *decomposition* of f, where $\circ$ denotes the composition of functions. A monomial x^d for $1 \leq d \leq n - 2$ is a permutation if and only if $\gcd(d, 2^n - 1) = 1$ and is called a *power permutation*. Further information about permutation polynomials can be found in [8].

Power permutations utilized to construct S-boxes in cryptography and the decomposition problem of such permutations into power permutations with lower degrees have a special interest considering efficient implementations in hardware [1,6]. Decomposition of power permutations is also important for TIs and side-channel countermeasures [2,4,7,12].

The degree of a permutation is defined as follows. Let $0 \leq i_1 < i_2 < \cdots < i_t \leq n - 2$ be integers for some $n > 2$ and $t > 1$. If a power permutation f over $\mathbb{F}_{2^n}$ can be expressed as

$$f(x) = x^{2^{i_1} + 2^{i_2} + \cdots + 2^{i_t}},$$

then t is called the *degree* of f. In particular, permutations with degree 2 are called *quadratic permutations*.

Carlitz showed in [3] that all permutation polynomials over $\mathbb{F}_q$, where $q > 2$, can be generated by the inversion x^{q-2} and affine polynomials $ax + b$. Therefore, the inversion mapping $x^{2^n - 2}$ has a further importance in cryptography under similar efficiency concerns.

Let us denote by $\mathcal{A}(k)$ the *cyclotomic class* of a power permutation x^k, namely

$$\mathcal{A}(k) := \{k \cdot 2^i \bmod (2^n - 1) :$$
$$\gcd(k \cdot 2^i, 2^n - 1) = 1 \text{ for } i = 0, \ldots, n - 1\}.$$

Nikova et al. presented an algorithm to decompose power permutations into quadratic power permutations in [9] using cyclotomic classes, see Algorithm 1.

We express that Step 1 in Algorithm 1 is the precomputation step and it exhaustively search for quadratic cyclotomic classes. We can decrease the memory complexity substantially if we apply Theorem 1 below.

Theorem 1 [10]. *If Step 1 of Algorithm 1 is replaced by command*

$$\mathcal{CP}_\mathcal{Q} = \{1 + 2^i : 1 \leq i \leq \lceil n/2 \rceil, \gcd(1 + 2^i, 2^n - 1) = 1\} \qquad (1)$$

then the output of the algorithm does not change.

The motivation behind Theorem 1 is to construct a set in which there are at least one representative from each cyclotomic class. The proof of Theorem 1 is based on the fact that

$$x^{1 + 2^{\lceil n/2 \rceil + u}} \equiv x^{2^{\lceil n/2 \rceil + u}} \circ x^{1 + 2^{\lfloor n/2 \rfloor - u}} \mod (x^{2^n} - x)$$

for some positive integer u. This fact means that there exists at least one element in the set in Eq. (1) from each cyclotomic class.

Remark 1. The precomputation and memory cost of both the adaptive and the exhaustive searches in Algorithm 1 are $2^n - 1$. On the other hand using Theorem 1 and Algorithm 2 given in [10], we need no precomputation step and the memory reduces to $\lceil n/2 \rceil$ numbers.

Algorithm 1: Algorithm of Decomposition into Quadratic Permutations in [9]

Input: Integers n and d.
Output: All quadratic decompositions of x^d over $\mathbb{F}_{2^n}[x]$.
1. First we build the set of all cyclotomic classes $\mathcal{A}(k)$, which are permutations and denote this set by $\mathcal{CP}$. Note that for any permutation x^d, the degree d will belong to only one cyclotomic class $\mathcal{A}(k) \in \mathcal{CP}$. Further, we consider the subset of $\mathcal{CP}$ consisting of quadratic permutations denoted by $\mathcal{CP}_{\mathcal{Q}}$.
2. For each k from $\mathcal{CP}_{\mathcal{Q}}$ compute the order of k as the smallest power m_k such that $wt(k^{m_k} \bmod (2^n - 1)) = 1$. In other words, x^{m_k} has algebraic degree 1, i.e. is a linear function. Hence, for each set $\mathcal{A}(k)$ we construct a corresponding set $\mathcal{P}(k)$ which we call the *power set* of k, namely
$\mathcal{P}(k) = \{k^i \bmod (2^n - 1) | i = 1, \ldots, m_k\}$. The collection of all power sets $\mathcal{P}(k)$ we denote by $\mathcal{P}$. Last define $l = |\mathcal{P}|$ and enumerate the representatives k of $\mathcal{P}(k) \in \mathcal{P}$ for example, k_i for $i = 1, \ldots, l$. Note 2 is not among them since it generates a linear permutation.
3. **Exhaustive Search:** For each $j_i = 0, \ldots, m_{k_i} - 1$ and $j = 0, \ldots, n - 1$ compute the number $z(j, j_1, \ldots, j_l) = 2^j \prod_{i=1}^{l} k_i^{j_i} \bmod (2^n - 1)$. Then check the condition $(\star)$, i.e. whether $z(j, j_1, \ldots, j_l) = d$. Note that the number $\sum_{i=1}^{l} j_i$ corresponds to the length of the decomposition. If the check $(\star)$ is satisfied then we remember the tuple $(j', j_1', \ldots, j_l')$ which results in the shorter decomposition length. Naturally at the end we have the decomposition with the shortest length. The complexity of this exhaustive search is $n \prod_{i=1}^{l} m_{k_i}$.
4. **Adaptive Search:** We start in the same way as in the exhaustive search i.e. for each $j_i = 0, \ldots, m_{k_i} - 1$ and $j = 0, \ldots, n - 1$, but with the additional constrain on the length of the decomposition, i.e. $\sum_{i=1}^{l} j_i \le t$ for a chosen t. However, when a tuple $(j', j_1', \ldots, j_l')$ is found which satisfies the check $(\star)$ and achieves a shorter decomposition length than the already known, then search space is reduced to only those tuples which have even shorter decomposition length.

---

3 A Complementary Result for Theorem 1

In this section, we investigate whether the set given in Theorem 1 can be reduced further. We formalize our problem as follows.

Problem 1. Find a systematic way to construct a set in which there is exactly one element from each quadratic cyclotomic class.

We present Theorem 2 below which proves that Theorem 1 is a solution for Problem 1.

Theorem 2. *For all $i, j, k \in \mathbb{Z}$ satisfying $1 \le i < j \le \frac{n}{2}$ and $0 \le k \le n - 1$, we have*

$$1 + 2^i \not\equiv (1 + 2^j)2^k \mod (2^n - 1). \tag{2}$$

Proof. Assume the contrary: Let there exist integers i, j and k satisfying $1 \le i < j \le \frac{n}{2}$, $0 \le k \le n - 1$ and Eq. (2). Then

$$2^{j+k} + 2^k - 2^i - 1 = (2^n - 1)l \tag{3}$$

for some $l \in \mathbb{Z}^+ \cup \{0\}$ (note that l cannot be negative since $0 < i < j$). We examine the rest in separate cases.

Case 1: Let $l = 0$, then $2^{j+k} + 2^k = 2^i + 1$. Since $2^k \ge 1$, we must have $2^i \ge 2^{j+k}$ and hence $i \ge j$. But this contradicts with the assumption that $i < j$.

Case 2: Let $l > 0$, then there exist unique $l_1, l_2, \ldots, l_m \in \mathbb{Z}$ satisfying $0 \le l_1 < l_2 < \cdots < l_m$ and $l = 2^{l_1} + \cdots + 2^{l_m}$. Thus

$$2^{j+k} + 2^k + 2^{l_1} + \cdots + 2^{l_m} = 1 + 2^i + 2^{n+l_1} + \cdots + 2^{n+l_m}. \tag{4}$$

Taking the right hand side of Eq. (4) into account, we use the notation $\min = 0$, $\min_0 = i$, $\min_1 = n + l_1$, $\ldots$, $\min_m = n + l_m$.

Case 2.1: Let $k = 0$, then $j \ge \max = n + l_m$ and hence $j \ge n$, which is a contradiction.

Case 2.2: Let $k > 0$, then $l_1 = 0$ since the right hand side is an odd number. Then

$$2^{j+k} + 2^k + 2^{l_2} + \cdots + 2^{l_m} = 2^i + 2^n + 2^{n+l_2} + \cdots + 2^{n+l_m}.$$

Case 2.2.1: Let $k = i$, then $\max = n + l_m \le j + i$. Thus $j + i \ge n$, which is a contradiction.

Case 2.2.2: Let $k \ne i$, then we must have $k > i$ and $l_2 = i$, since the equation must be kept when we take modulo 2^{i+1}. Then

$$2^{j+k} + 2^k + 2^{l_3} + \cdots + 2^{l_m} = 2^n + 2^{n+l_2} + \cdots + 2^{n+l_m}.$$

Here, the terms of the right hand side are all distinct, therefore the right hand side is in the base 2 representation. On the other hand, the number of terms on the left hand side is equal to the number of terms on the right hand side, which means that all the terms on the left hand side are all distinct, too (otherwise, the number of terms of the base 2 representation of the left hand side will decrease). Here, the smallest term on the right hand side is 2^n whereas the smallest term on the left hand side is smaller than 2^n since $k < n$. This is a contradiction again. □

Remark 2. We would like to emphasize that the proof of Theorem 2 is based on some elementary tools and presented compactly.

4 Conclusion

The problem of decomposition of power permutations into quadratic power permutations over finite fields $\mathbb{F}_{2^n}$, motivated from the applications to cryptography, was investigated by Nikova et al. in [9]. The memory cost of the precomputation step of the algorithm in [9] was substantially reduced by Otal and Tekin in [10]. In this paper, we proved that this reduction cannot be improved further; in that way, we complemented the solution in [10].

References

1. Bilgin, B., Nikova, S., Nikov, V., Rijmen, V., Tokareva, N., Vitkup, V.: Threshold implementations of small S-boxes. Cryptogr. Commun. **7**(1), 3–33 (2014). https://doi.org/10.1007/s12095-014-0104-7
2. Carlet, C., Prouff, E., Rivain, M., Roche, T.: Algebraic decomposition for probing security. In: Gennaro, R., Robshaw, M. (eds.) CRYPTO 2015. LNCS, vol. 9215, pp. 742–763. Springer, Heidelberg (2015). https://doi.org/10.1007/978-3-662-47989-6_36
3. Carlitz, L.: Permutations in a finite field. Proc. Amer. Math. Soc. **4**(538), 1 (1953)
4. Coron, J.-S., Roy, A., Vivek, S.: Fast evaluation of polynomials over binary finite fields and application to side-channel countermeasures. J. Cryptogr. Eng. **5**(2), 73–83 (2015). https://doi.org/10.1007/s13389-015-0099-9
5. Çomak, P., Özbudak, F.: On the parity of power permutations. IEEE Access **9**, 106806–106812 (2021). https://doi.org/10.1109/ACCESS.2021.3097914
6. Daemen, J., Rijmen, R.: The Design of Rijndael: AES - The Advanced Encryption Standard. Information Security and Cryptography, Springer, Heidelberg (2002). https://doi.org/10.1007/978-3-662-04722-4
7. Kutzner, S., Nguyen, P.H., Poschmann, A.: Enabling 3-share threshold implementations for all 4-bit S-boxes. In: Lee, H.-S., Han, D.-G. (eds.) ICISC 2013. LNCS, vol. 8565, pp. 91–108. Springer, Cham (2014). https://doi.org/10.1007/978-3-319-12160-4_6
8. Lidl, R., Niederreiter, H.: Finite Fields, vol. 20. Cambridge University Press, Cambridge (1997)
9. Nikova, S., Nikov, V., Rijmen, V.: Decomposition of permutations in a finite field. Cryptogr. Commun. **11**(3), 379–384 (2018). https://doi.org/10.1007/s12095-018-0317-2
10. Otal, K., Tekin, E.: Efficient generation of quadratic cyclotomic classes for shortest quadratic decompositions of polynomials. Cryptogr. Commun. **13**(5), 837–845 (2021). https://doi.org/10.1007/s12095-021-00512-z
11. Ouladj, M., Guilley, S.: Side-Channel Analysis of Embedded Systems: An Efficient Algorithmic Approach. Springer, Heidelberg (2021). https://doi.org/10.1007/978-3-030-77222-2
12. Poschmann, A., Moradi, A., Khoo, K., Lim, C.-W., Wang, H., Ling, S.: Side-channel resistant crypto for less than 2,300 GE. J. Cryptol. **24**(2), 322–345 (2010). https://doi.org/10.1007/s00145-010-9086-6

A Framework for the Design of Secure and Efficient Proofs of Retrievability

Françoise Levy-dit-Vehel[1] and Maxime Roméas[2(✉)]

[1] LIX, ENSTA Paris, INRIA, Institut Polytechnique de Paris,
91120 Palaiseau, France
levy@ensta.fr
[2] LIX, École Polytechnique, INRIA, Institut Polytechnique de Paris,
91120 Palaiseau, France
romeas@lix.polytechnique.fr

Abstract. Proofs of Retrievability (PoR) protocols ensure that a client can fully retrieve a large outsourced file from an untrusted server. Good PoRs should have low communication complexity, small storage overhead and clear security guarantees with tight security bounds. The focus of this work is to design good PoR schemes with simple security proofs. To this end, we propose a framework for the design of secure and efficient PoR schemes that is based on Locally Correctable Codes, and whose security is phrased in the Constructive Cryptography model by Maurer. We give a first instantiation of our framework using the high rate lifted codes introduced by Guo *et al*. This yields an infinite family of good PoRs. We assert their security by solving a finite geometry problem, giving an explicit formula for the probability of an adversary to fool the client. Moreover, we show that the security of a PoR of Lavauzelle and Levy-dit-Vehel was overestimated and propose new secure parameters for it. Finally, using the local correctability properties of Tanner codes, we get another instantiation of our framework and derive an analogous formula for the success probability of the audit.

1 Introduction

1.1 Context and State-of-the-Art

With the continuous increase in data creation, individuals and business entities call upon remote storage providers to outsource their data. This new dependency raises some issues, as the storage provider can try to read and/or modify the client's data. Besides, when a client does not often access his data, the service provider can delete it to make room for another client's data. In this context, it appears important to deploy client side protections designed to bring security guarantees like confidentiality and integrity. In this work, we focus on the following problem: given a client who stored a file on a server and erased its local copy, how can he check if he is able to retrieve his file from the server in full? Addressing this issue is the goal of a class of cryptographic protocols called Proofs of Retrievability (PoRs).

A. Nitaj and K. Zkik (Eds.): I4CS 2022, CCIS 1747, pp. 83–103, 2022.
https://doi.org/10.1007/978-3-031-23201-5_6

The first PoR scheme was proposed in 2007 by Juels and Kaliski [8] and was based on checking the integrity of some sentinel symbols secretly placed by the client before uploading its file. This scheme has low communication but its drawback is that it is bounded-use only, as the number of possible verifications depends on the number of sentinels. To correct this drawback, Shacham and Waters [15] proposed to append some authenticator symbols to the file. Verification consists in checking random linear combinations of file symbols and authenticators. Then comes a few PoR schemes based on codes. Bowers *et al.* [2] proposed a double-layer encoding with the use of an inner code to recover information symbols and an outer code to correct the remaining erasures. Dodis *et al.* [4] formalize the verification process as a request to a code which models the space of possible answers to a challenge. They use Reed-Solomon codes to design their PoR scheme. In 2013, Paterson *et al.* [14] laid the foundation for studying PoR schemes using a coding theoretic framework. Following these ideas, Lavauzelle and Levy-dit-Vehel [11] (2016) used the local structure of the lifted codes introduced by Guo *et al.* [5] to build a PoR scheme, that compares favourably to those presented above w.r.t. storage overhead.

Unfortunately, PoR schemes have a few issues. Indeed, their security definitions are often unclear, making it hard to understand what they really achieve. Moreover, when a client wants to retrieve his data, the security guarantees brought by the use of the PoR scheme only holds under the condition that both client and server unveil some private information (client's secret material and server's state). We give a detailed explanation of this in Sect. 2.2. In 2018, Badertscher and Maurer [1] used the Constructive Cryptography (CC) model [12] to propose a new PoR definition, that avoids the aforementioned flaws. They also designed a PoR scheme based on generic erasure codes. Generalizing [1] and [11], we introduce a framework for designing secure, composable and efficient PoR protocols based on locally correctable codes.

Our approach allows us to design and study the security of PoR schemes in a modular fashion, that achieves stronger security and clearer security guarantees than previous schemes (whose security was based on so-called ϵ adversaries or related notions). Using another definitional model such as the Universal Composability one by Canetti [3] would probably give closely related results. We chose to use CC because it makes the resources available to the parties (namely, untrusted server storage, local memories, communication channels) explicit. It also makes the switching between computational, statistical and information-theoretic security notions easy.

Locally correctable codes (LCCs), which are at the core of our work, were formally introduced by Katz and Trevisan [9] in 2000. Reed-Muller codes are well known to be locally correctable, but with poor rate as their length grows. The year 2011 has seen a breakthrough in the theory of codes with locality, with the construction by Kopparty *et al.* [10] of a class of high-rate LCCs -the multiplicity codes- generalizing the Reed-Muller class. Other high-rate LCCs are notably the lifted codes introduced by Guo *et al.* [5], and the expander codes of Hemenway *et al.* [6]. The high rates of these codes permit to minimize the server storage overhead, making them best suited for the outsourced storage context.

We give an instantiation of our framework using the lifted codes of Guo *et al.* In a nutshell, we exploit the geometric properties of lifted codes and the CC security model for PoRs to give simple security proofs with tight bounds. This is a key difference between our approach and the one of Lavauzelle and Levy-dit-Vehel [11], which is also based on lifted codes and can in fact be seen as a different instantiation of our framework. We also propose another instantiation of our framework using the graph codes of Tanner [16].

1.2 Contributions

Given a LCC, we propose a canvas for deriving a PoR scheme. We get efficiency by taking advantage of the local correctability of the code to design an audit with low communication complexity. Using the CC security model for PoRs of [1], we give clear and composable security guarantees for our PoR construction. We are also able to give security bounds derived from geometric/combinatorial proofs and we reevaluate the security of the scheme of [11].

As in many protocols, the client first encodes its file and uploads it to the server. Retrieving the file is done by iterating the local decoder. With such a decoding process in mind, for extracting the file, we identify the adversarial configurations of corruptions that would prevent its extraction. This analysis of adversarial impact permits us to phrase the security of the audit -which heavily relies on the local correction step- as a problem about the structure of the code. Namely, if the code uses geometric properties of $\mathbb{F}_q^m$, we reduce the security of the audit to a finite geometry problem that we thoroughly address in Sect. 5.2. If the code is a graph code, we reduce the security to a graph theoretic problem in Sect. 5.3.

Instantiating our Framework with the Lifted Reed-Solomon Codes: we characterize all the configurations of corruptions that are impossible to correct using the local correctability of those codes. More precisely, we show that these configurations of corruptions correspond to sets of points verifying a geometric property inside a vector space over a finite field. Then, we show that these sets of points belong to a large number of affine lines. From this we derive an explicit formula for the probability of the adversary to fool the client. Thus, we get a family of PoR schemes with precise security guarantees. Efficiency of this construction is shown in Fig. 6 and 7 of Sect. 6, where we also give a comparison between our parameters and those of the PoR scheme of [11]. Our security analysis shows that their scheme is insecure for their choice of parameters. Fortunately, we are able to give new ranges of secure parameters in Fig. 6.

Instantiating Our Framework with Tanner Codes: we proceed analogously as in the lifted Reed-Solomon codes case to first design a global decoder, and then to characterize the configurations of erased edges that are unrecoverable by the decoding algorithm. This way, we derive a bound for the failure probability of the audit, that only depends on the choice of the graph.

In order to design our framework, we constructed a protocol to authenticate outsourced data (**aSMR**, for Authentic Server Memory Resource[1]) that is

---

[1] Following the terminology of [1].

tailored for PoR purposes (see Sect. 4). Our **aSMR** is different from the one of [1] in several aspects, notably, when dealing with encoded data, we halve the extra storage needed in comparison to [1]. Further details are to be found in Sect. 4. This new construction might be useful in other code-based schemes. It can also be used to improve the efficiency of the generic PoR of [1].

2   Background

2.1   The Constructive Cryptography Model

The CC model, introduced by Maurer [13] in 2011, aims at asserting the real security of cryptographic primitives. To do so, it redefines them in terms of so-called *resources* and *converters*. In this model, starting from a basic resource (e.g. communication channel, shared key, memory server...), a converter (a cryptographic protocol) aims at constructing an enhanced resource, *i.e.*, one with better security guarantees. The starting resource, lacking the desired security guarantees, is often called the *real* resource and the obtained one is often called the *ideal* resource, since it does not exist as is in the real world. An example of ideal resource is a confidential server, where the data stored by a client is readable by this client only. The only information that leaks to other parties is its length. This resource does not exist, but it can be emulated by an insecure server on which the client uses a suitable encryption protocol. We say that this *construction* of the confidential server is secure if the adversary in the ideal world, *i.e.* when a confidential server is used, is able to do the same things than in the real world setting, *i.e.* when an insecure server is used together with the protocol. We use the fact that the ideal world is by definition secure and contraposition to conclude. This construction notion is illustrated in Fig. 2.

The CC model follows a top-down approach, allowing to get rid of superfluous hypotheses made in other models. A particularity of this model is its composability, in the sense that a protocol obtained by composition of a number of secure constructions is itself secure. We give the required material to understand how we use CC below. We follow the presentation of [7].

Resources, Converters and Distinguishers. A *resource* **R** is a system that interacts, in a black-box manner, at one or more of its *interfaces*, by receiving an input at a given interface and subsequently sending an output at the same interface. Do note that a resource only defines the observable behavior of a system and not how it is defined internally.

In CC, *converters* are used to link resources and reprogram interfaces, thus expressing the local computations of the parties involved. A converter is plugged in a set of interfaces at the inside and provides a set of interfaces at the outside. When it receives an input at its outside interface, the converter uses a bounded number of queries to the inside interface before computing a value and outputting it at its outside interface. A converter π connected to the interface set $\mathcal{I}$ of a resource **R** yields a new resource $\mathbf{R}' := \pi^{\mathcal{I}}\mathbf{R}$. The interfaces of $\mathbf{R}'$ inside the set $\mathcal{I}$ are the interfaces emulated by π. A protocol can be modeled as a tuple of converters with pairwise disjoint interface sets.

A *distinguisher* $\mathbf{D}$ is an environment that connects to all interfaces of a resource $\mathbf{R}$ and sends queries to them. At any point, the distinguisher can end its interaction by outputting a bit. Its advantage is defined as $\Delta^{\mathbf{D}}(\mathbf{R}, \mathbf{S}) := |\Pr[\mathbf{D}(\mathbf{R}) = 1] - \Pr[\mathbf{D}(\mathbf{S}) = 1]|$.

In this work, we make statements about resources with interface sets of the form $\mathcal{I} := \mathcal{P} \cup \{\mathsf{S}, \mathsf{W}\}$, where $\mathcal{P} := \{\mathsf{C_0}, \mathsf{C}\}$ is the set of honest client interfaces. A protocol is a pair of converters $\pi := (\pi_{\mathsf{C_0}}, \pi_{\mathsf{C}})$ that specifies one converter for each interface. The goal of this protocol is to construct a so-called ideal resource from an available real resource in presence of a potentially dishonest server S. The world interface W models the direct influence of a distinguisher on a resource.

Specifications. In CC, systems are grouped according to desired or assumed properties that are relevant to the user, while other properties are ignored on purpose. A *specification* $\mathcal{S}$ is a set of resources that have the same interface set and share some properties, for example confidentiality. In order to construct this set of confidential resources, one can use a specification of assumed resources $\mathcal{R}$ and a protocol π, and show that the specification $\pi\mathcal{R}$ satisfies confidentiality. Proving security is thus proving that $\pi\mathcal{R} \subseteq \mathcal{S}$, sometimes written as $\mathcal{R} \xrightarrow{\pi} \mathcal{S}$, and we say that the protocol π constructs the specification $\mathcal{S}$ from the specification $\mathcal{R}$. The composition property of the framework comes from the transitivity of inclusion. Formally, for specifications $\mathcal{R}, \mathcal{S}$ and $\mathcal{T}$ and protocols π for $\mathcal{R}$ and π' for $\mathcal{S}$, we have $\mathcal{R} \xrightarrow{\pi} \mathcal{S} \wedge \mathcal{S} \xrightarrow{\pi'} \mathcal{T} \Rightarrow \mathcal{R} \xrightarrow{\pi' \circ \pi} \mathcal{T}$.

We use the real-world/ideal-world paradigm, and often refer to $\pi\mathcal{R}$ and $\mathcal{S}$ as the real and ideal-world specifications respectively, to understand security statements. Those statements say that the real-world is "just as good" as the ideal one, meaning that it does not matter whether parties interact with an arbitrary element of $\pi\mathcal{R}$ or one of $\mathcal{S}$. This means that the guarantees of the ideal specification $\mathcal{S}$ also apply in the real world where an assumed resource is used together with the protocol.

We use *simulators*, *i.e.*, converters that translate behaviors of the real world to the ideal world, to make the achieved security guarantees obvious. For example, one can model confidential servers as a specification $\mathcal{S}$ that only leaks the data length, combined with some simulator σ, and show that $\pi\mathcal{R} \subseteq \sigma\mathcal{S}$. It is then clear that the adversary cannot learn anything more that the data length.

Server-Memory Resources. We recall the constructions of [1] that we will use or improve in this work. The first resource is the basic server-memory resource (SMR) denoted by $\mathbf{SMR}_{\Sigma,n}$ where Σ is the alphabet and n is the number of data blocks. It allows a client to read and write data blocks that are encoded as elements of a finite alphabet Σ via interface C. The interface $\mathsf{C_0}$ is used to set up the initial state of the resource. The server can be "honest but curious" by obtaining the entire history of accesses made by the client (a log file) and reading its data at interface S_H. The server can also be intrusive and overwrite data using its interface S_I when the resource is set into a special write mode. This write mode can be toggled by the distinguisher at the world interface W. The specification of the resource $\mathbf{SMR}_{\Sigma,n}$ is given in Fig. 1.

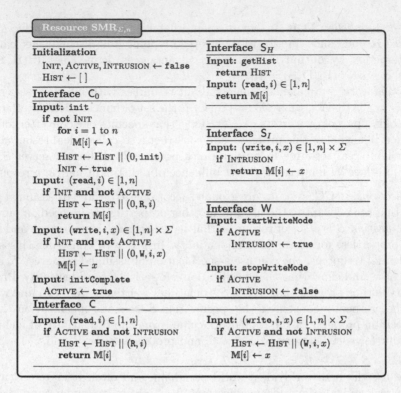

Fig. 1. Description of the basic server-memory resource

In Fig. 2, taken from [1], we illustrate the CC construction notion on SMRs. The SMR security guarantees can be augmented to provide authenticity by using a suitable protocol in this construction notion. This new SMR is called authentic SMR, denoted by $\mathbf{aSMR}_{\Sigma,n}$, and is constructed in [1]. In $\mathbf{aSMR}$, the behavior of the server at interface S_I is weakened as the server cannot modify the content of data blocks but is limited to either delete or restore previously deleted data blocks. A deleted data block is indicated by the special symbol ϵ. In this work, we use a different $\mathbf{aSMR}$ specification that the one used in [1]. We modify the `restore` behavior to only restore data blocks that were deleted after the last client update of the database. We introduce a version number that tracks the number of said updates in the history of the $\mathbf{aSMR}$ and the client is now allowed to overwrite corrupted data blocks. These changes decrease the storage overhead along with the communication complexity of read operations while the communication complexity of write operations is increased in comparison to the specification of [1]. Our changes to the $\mathbf{aSMR}$ yield substantial improvements for the parameters of our code-based PoR schemes. Our take on the $\mathbf{aSMR}$ resource is described in Fig. 3 and our changes are precised in Sect. 4.

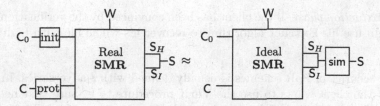

Fig. 2. Illustration of the construction notion for SMRs. On the left, we have a real **SMR** with a protocol for the client. On the right, we have an ideal **SMR** with stronger security guarantees. The construction is secure if there exists a simulator that makes these two resources indistinguishable.

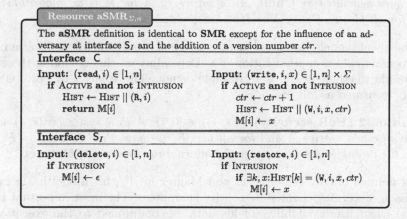

Fig. 3. Our new authentic SMR (only the differences with **SMR** are shown)

2.2   Proofs of Retrievability

Proofs of Retrievability (PoR) are cryptographic protocols whose goal is to guarantee that a file stored by a client on a server remains retrievable in full. PoRs thus involve two parties: a client who owns a file F and a server, here modeled as a SMR, on which F is stored. We recall the commonly used definitions for PoR security as presented in [11]. A PoR scheme is composed of three main procedures:

- *An initialization phase.* The client encodes his file F with an initialization function $\mathbf{Init}(F) = (\tilde{F}, \mathtt{data})$. He keeps $\mathtt{data}$ (*e.g.* keys, etc.) for himself, then he sends $\tilde{F}$ to the server and erases F.
- *A verification phase.* The client produces a challenge c with a randomized **Chall** function and sends it to the server. The latter creates a response $r = \mathbf{Resp}(\tilde{F}, c)$ and sends it back to the client. The client checks if r is correct by running $\mathbf{Verif}(c, r)$, which also access $\mathtt{data}$, and outputs $\mathtt{accept}$ if r is considered correct and $\mathtt{reject}$ otherwise.

- *An extraction phase.* If the client has been convinced by the verification phase, he can use his **Extract** algorithm to recover his whole file with high probability.

The security of PoR schemes is usually defined with ϵ-adversaries. In a PoR scheme, the client wants to use the **Verif** procedure to be sure that he will be able to retrieve his file in full when using the **Extract** procedure. The following definition models the fact that, if the server's answers to client's challenges make him "look like" he owns the file, then the client must be able to recover it entirely.

Definition 1 (ϵ-adversary). *Let $\mathcal{P}$ be a PoR system and X be the space of challenges generated by* **Chall**. *An ϵ-adversary $\mathcal{A}$ for $\mathcal{P}$ is an algorithm such that, for all files F, $\Pr_{x \in X}[\mathbf{Verif}(x, \mathcal{A}(x)) = \mathtt{false}] \leq \epsilon$.*

The client models the server as an ϵ-adversary and uses his verification process to maintain an approximation of ϵ. Depending on this estimate, the client can decide whether his file is retrievable or not. The security of PoRs is thus usually measured as follows:

Definition 2 (PoR security). *Let $\epsilon, \rho \in [0, 1]$. A PoR system is (ϵ, ρ)-sound if, for all ϵ-adversaries $\mathcal{A}$ and for all files F, we have $\Pr[\mathbf{Extract}^{\mathcal{A}} = F] \geq \rho$ where the probability is taken over the internal randomness of $\mathbf{Extract}^{\mathcal{A}}$.*

As pointed out by Badertscher and Maurer in [1], this model has a major drawback concerning client-side security guarantees. The most important thing for the client, the availability of his data, is conditioned to the execution of the **Extract** algorithm which needs to access the client's private data and the server's strategy (as indicated in Definition 2). In practice, no server would reveal its entire state to a client. This problem is addressed in [1], where the authors used the CC framework to propose a definition of PoRs that fixes this drawback. In their work, they introduced an ideal abstraction of PoRs in the form of an ideal SMR that sees the client's interface augmented with an `audit` mechanism. On an `audit` request, the resource checks whether the current memory content is indeed the newest version that the client wrote to the storage. If a single data block has changed, the ideal audit will detect this and output `reject` to the client. In case of a successful audit (returning `accept`), this guarantee holds until the server gains write-access to the storage, in which case a new audit has to reveal whether modifications have been made. We present the specification of the auditable and authentic SMR $\mathbf{aSMR}_{\Sigma,n}^{\mathtt{audit}}$ in Fig. 4. In addition to the advantages we discussed, we believe that this CC based security model is simpler and more intuitive than the one of ϵ-adversaries.

In CC, a PoR scheme is given by a pair of converters $\mathsf{por} := (\mathsf{por}_{\mathsf{init}}, \mathsf{por}_{\mathsf{audit}})$ where $\mathsf{por}_{\mathsf{init}}$ implements the $(\mathtt{write}, F)$ query that uploads F (or an encoded/encrypted version of F) on the SMR, where F is the client's file and $\mathsf{por}_{\mathsf{audit}}$ implements the `audit` query that returns either `accept` or `reject`, and the `read` query that extracts the file F from the SMR.

2.3 Locally Correctable Codes

In [1], Badertscher and Maurer give a protocol based on generic erasure codes to construct the auditable **aSMR**. Due to the use of classical codes, a client who wants to read a single data block needs to read the entire memory in order for him to run the decoding algorithm of the code to recover (or not) the data block. In this work, we show how one can use LCCs, so that one has to read only a small number of memory positions to recover one data block, while keeping the auditable property of the constructed resource. We now briefly present LCCs, which were formally introduced by Katz and Trevisan [9] in 2000.

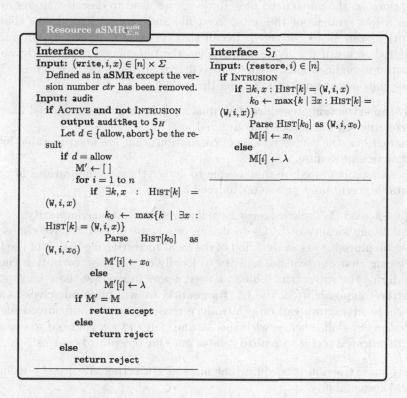

Resource aSMR$_{\Sigma,n}^{\text{audit}}$

Interface C

Input: $(\texttt{write}, i, x) \in [n] \times \Sigma$
    Defined as in **aSMR** except the version number ctr has been removed.
Input: audit
    if ACTIVE **and not** INTRUSION
        output auditReq to S_H
        Let $d \in \{\text{allow}, \text{abort}\}$ be the result
        if $d = \text{allow}$
            $M' \leftarrow [\,]$
            for $i = 1$ **to** n
                if $\exists k, x : \text{HIST}[k] = (\texttt{W}, i, x)$
                    $k_0 \leftarrow \max\{k \mid \exists x : \text{HIST}[k] = (\texttt{W}, i, x)\}$
                    Parse $\text{HIST}[k_0]$ as $(\texttt{W}, i, x_0)$
                    $M'[i] \leftarrow x_0$
                else
                    $M'[i] \leftarrow \lambda$
            if $M' = M$
                return accept
            else
                return reject
        else
            return reject

Interface S_I

Input: $(\texttt{restore}, i) \in [n]$
    if INTRUSION
        if $\exists k, x : \text{HIST}[k] = (\texttt{W}, i, x)$
            $k_0 \leftarrow \max\{k \mid \exists x : \text{HIST}[k] = (\texttt{W}, i, x)\}$
            Parse $\text{HIST}[k_0]$ as $(\texttt{W}, i, x_0)$
            $M[i] \leftarrow x_0$
         else
            $M[i] \leftarrow \lambda$

Fig. 4. Description of the auditable and authentic SMR of [1] (only the differences with our **aSMR** are shown)

Definition 3 (Locally correctable code). *Let $r \in \mathbb{N}, \delta \in [0, 1]$ and $\epsilon : [0, 1] \to [0, 1]$. A code $\mathcal{C} \subseteq \mathbb{F}_q^n$ is said to be (r, δ, ϵ)-locally correctable if there exists a probabilistic decoding algorithm $\mathcal{A}$ such that,*

1. For all $\mathbf{c} \in \mathcal{C}$, for all $i \in [\![1, n]\!]$ and for all vectors $\mathbf{y} \in \mathbb{F}_q^n$ with relative Hamming distance $\Delta(\mathbf{c}, \mathbf{y}) \leq \delta$, we have $\Pr[\mathcal{A}^{\mathbf{y}}(i) = \mathbf{c}_i] \geq 1 - \epsilon(\delta)$, where the probability is taken over the internal randomness of $\mathcal{A}^{\mathbf{y}}$.

2. *The algorithm $\mathcal{A}$ makes at most r queries to the vector $\mathbf{y}$.*

In this work, we consider locally correctable codes for erasures and we do not use the estimate of their failure probability. See Sect. 3 for more details.

3   Our Framework

We describe our framework which derives PoR schemes from a given LCC $\mathcal{C}$. In all our PoRs, the client's file is encoded as a codeword of $\mathcal{C}$ and uploaded to the server. We want to protect the client from an adversary able to introduce corruptions on the outsourced file. To do so, we need to describe an audit that probes a few symbols of the outsourced file and accepts if it thinks that the corruptions can all be corrected. Recall that, in the CC definition, an audit is considered secure if it only succeeds when the outsourced file is retrievable in full, without modifications. If we want to derive PoR schemes from an LCC $\mathcal{C}$ in CC, we thus need to do the following three things:

1. Give an extraction procedure that aims at retrieving the outsourced file while correcting any corruption encountered.
2. Characterize the configurations of corruptions that are uncorrectable by this extraction procedure.
3. Give an audit procedure that is able to detect those configurations of uncorrectable corruptions on the outsourced file.

Since a good PoR scheme must have low communication complexity, we want to exploit the locality of LCCs to design our audit procedure. We choose our extraction procedure as an iteration of the local correction algorithm of the LCC. This means that our schemes will try to locally correct any corruption encountered during the extraction. Thus, we need a way to identify those corruptions. Using the composability of the CC framework, we will place ourselves in a setting where adversaries can only introduce erasures on the outsourced file. We can design our PoR schemes with this assumption and we will need to construct an authenticated server to realize it later on. Our blueprint becomes:

1. Give an extraction procedure that aims at correcting erasures by using the local correctability of $\mathcal{C}$.
2. Characterize the configurations of erasures that are uncorrectable by this extraction procedure.
3. Our audit is the following: try to locally correct a random position of the outsourced file, if the correction is impossible return reject, else return accept.

In step 2, we identify the configurations of erasures that are unrecoverable when iterating the local correction of $\mathcal{C}$. We find a lower bound on the number of local correction queries that would fail if such a configuration of erasures existed. When instantiating our framework in Sect. 5, we shall see that this problem is, in practice, much easier than giving a lower bound on the minimum size of such a configuration of unrecoverable erasures. In the CC model of security for PoRs, the advantage of the adversary in breaking the security of the scheme is the probability that the audit accepts while the file is not retrievable. In our case, our audit consists in checking if a random local correction query succeeds. Our file is not retrievable if there exists a configuration of unrecoverable erasures. Thus, the lower bound we computed above is all we need to assess the security of the PoR. We give a complete proof when instantiating our framework, see Theorem 1 of Sect. 5.

More precisely, let $\mathcal{C}$ be an erasure code of length n, alphabet Σ and erasure symbol $\bot$. Suppose that $\mathcal{C}$ possesses a local erasure decoder $\mathcal{L}$ with query space $\mathcal{Q} \subseteq 2^{[1,n]}$. On query $q \in \mathcal{Q}$ and input $w \in (\Sigma \cup \{\bot\})^n$ such that there exists $c \in \mathcal{C}$ such that for any $i \in [1, n]$, $w_i \neq \bot$ implies $w_i = c_i$, $\mathcal{L}$ probes the symbols $w_{|q} := (w_i)_{i \in q}$ of w and attempts to correct its erasures if they exist. We can define a global decoder $\mathcal{G}$ for $\mathcal{C}$ by iterating $\mathcal{L}$ until no erasures remain. Let P be a predicate on $\cup_{i=0}^n (\Sigma \cup \{\bot\})^i$, $i.e.$, for $w \in (\Sigma \cup \{\bot\})^n$ and $q \in \mathcal{Q}$, $P(w_{|q}) \in \{\text{true, false}\}$. Let $0 \leq \epsilon \leq 1$ and suppose that we have the following property:

$$\forall w \in (\Sigma \cup \{\bot\})^n, \text{if at least one erasure of } w \text{ cannot be corrected by } \mathcal{G}$$
$$\text{then } \Pr_{q \in \mathcal{Q}}[P(w_{|q}) = \text{false}] \geq 1 - \epsilon \quad (1)$$

We define our general PoR scheme $\mathsf{por} := (\mathsf{por}_{\mathsf{init}}, \mathsf{por}_{\mathsf{audit}})$, where:

1. On input $(\mathtt{write}, F)$, $\mathsf{por}_{\mathsf{init}}$ encodes F into a codeword $\tilde{F}$ of $\mathcal{C}$ and writes $\tilde{F}$ in the **aSMR** memory.
2. On input $\mathtt{audit}$, $\mathsf{por}_{\mathsf{audit}}$ samples a query $q \in \mathcal{Q}$ uniformly. If w is the file stored in the SMR, $\mathsf{por}_{\mathsf{audit}}$ retrieves $w_{|q}$ with **read** queries. Then, the converter returns $\mathtt{accept}$ if $P(w_{|q} = \text{true})$ and returns $\mathtt{reject}$ otherwise.
3. On input $(\mathtt{read})$, the converter $\mathsf{por}_{\mathsf{audit}}$ tries to extract the file F using the global decoder $\mathcal{G}$ of $\mathcal{C}$.

Recall that in the CC model of security for PoRs, the advantage of the adversary in breaking the security of por is the probability that the audit accepts while the file is not retrievable. In our case, this advantage is upper bounded by ϵ (see Eq. 1). We believe our security model for PoRs to be cleaner, simpler and to give clearer security guarantees than the ϵ-adversary model.

4   Our Authentication Protocol

Recall that we focus on schemes based on erasure capabilities of error correcting codes. Thus, we need a setting where the actions of adversaries only lead to introducing erasures, instead of errors, in the outsourced data. This is exactly what an authentic server-memory resource (**aSMR**) achieves since the adversary can only delete data or restore previously deleted data. Thus, we need a protocol that constructs an **aSMR** from a basic **SMR**.

In [1], Badertscher and Maurer present a protocol that constructs an **aSMR** using a MAC function, timestamps and a tree structure on the outsourced data. Their construction of the **aSMR** has the following features:

1. The **aSMR** of size n with alphabet Σ is constructed from an **SMR** of size $2n - 1$, alphabet $\Sigma \times \mathbb{Z}_q \times \mathcal{T}$ and a local memory of constant size for the client. $\mathcal{T}$ is the tag space of the MAC function used.
2. To read or write one memory cell on **aSMR**, the protocol of [1] produces $O(\log n)$ read and write queries to **SMR**.

Our work focuses on PoR schemes where the client uploads a very large encoded file to an outsourced server. In this context, the logarithm of the size of the alphabet Σ is an order of magnitude smaller than the length of the MAC tags. The **aSMR** construction of [1] is thus not suited for this kind of application. Its issues are threefold. First, since the file size is huge, a factor of 2 in the storage overhead is a big problem. Second, the $O(\log n)$ communication complexity for write operations is of no use to us since we will be working on encoded data and updating a codeword requires anyway to read a linear number of symbols. Third, the verification phase of PoRs often consists in probing as few symbols as possible to ensure that the outsourced file is retrievable in full. Having a $O(\log n)$ read communication complexity is a problem in this context.

With these observations, we now present a different protocol that constructs an **aSMR** with good features for our context:

1. Our **aSMR** of size n with alphabet Σ is constructed using an **SMR** of size n, alphabet $\Sigma \times \mathcal{T}$ and a local memory of constant size for the client.
2. A read request to our **aSMR** produces only one read request to **SMR**.
3. A write request to our **aSMR** produces at most $2n - 1$ read and write requests to **SMR**.

This way, we minimize the storage overhead and the communication complexity of read requests on the one hand. On the other hand, the increased communication complexity for write requests does not matter since our PoR schemes use only one such request. We sketch our protocol.

In the following, let n be the size of the **SMR**, $f_{sk}(\cdot)$ be a MAC function with tag space $\mathcal{T}$ and Σ be a finite alphabet. The protocol auth starts with the clients choosing a secret key sk for the MAC function, setting a version number ctr to 0. The main idea is the following: if the i-th cell is supposed to store the data $x \in \Sigma$, the protocol will store the pair $(x, f_{sk}(x, ctr, i)) \in \Sigma \times \mathcal{T}$ instead. Do note that the version number ctr is incremented with every write request. This also means that every valid tag needs to be updated with every write request. Intuitively, this protocol prevents the adversary from:

1. Replacing the data x with $y \neq x$ since this would make the tag invalid.
2. Moving the data stored in location i to location $j \neq i$ since this would make the tag invalid.
3. Replaying an older value since the version numbers would not match and the tag would thus be invalid.

5 Instantiation with High Rate LCCs

5.1 Lifted Reed-Solomon Codes

We introduce a very interesting class of LCCs, namely the high rate lifted Reed-Solomon (RS) codes of Guo *et al.* [5]. In the following, let $\mathbb{F}_q$ be the finite field with q elements and m be a positive integer. The set of affine lines in $\mathbb{F}_q^m$ is denoted by $\mathcal{L}_m := \{(at + b)_{t \in \mathbb{F}_q} \mid a, b \in \mathbb{F}_q^m\}$. $\mathrm{RS}_q[q, d]$ is the q-ary RS code of length q and minimum distance $d = q - k + 1$.

Definition 4 (Lifted Reed-Solomon Code [5]). *Let $\mathbb{F}_q$ be a finite field. Let $d, m \in \mathbb{N}^*$. The m-lift of $\mathrm{RS}_q[q, d]$ is $\mathrm{Lift}_m(\mathrm{RS}_q[q, d]) := \{w \in (\mathbb{F}_q)^{q^m} \mid \forall \text{ line } \ell \subseteq \mathbb{F}_q^m, w_{|\ell} \in \mathrm{RS}_q[q, d]\}$.*

As we are using an **aSMR**, codewords can only be affected by potential erasures. A codeword of the RS base code $\mathrm{RS}_q[q, d]$ is the vector of evaluations of a polynomial f of degree strictly less than $k = q - d + 1$. Thus, if there are at most $d - 1$ erasures, we can always recover the codeword *i.e.* the polynomial f by interpolating on $k > \deg f$ points. Therefore, if we want to correct a coordinate $x \in \mathbb{F}_q^m$ of the $\mathrm{Lift}_m(\mathrm{RS}_q[q, d])$ code, we can pick a random line going through x and run the aforementioned local decoding algorithm.

5.2 The Lifted RS PoR Scheme

In this section, we use our PoR framework to design a secure and efficient PoR scheme using lifted RS erasure codes. We call this scheme *lifted RS PoR scheme*. We build our PoR for an **aSMR** and then use the composability of CC. Since this server is authenticated, we only have to deal with potential erasures instead of errors. Using the blueprint of Sect. 3, we need to do the following:

1. Give a global decoding algorithm for lifted RS codes using their local correctability.
2. Characterize the configurations of erasures that are unrecoverable by this algorithm.
3. Give an audit procedure that is able to detect those configurations of uncorrectable corruptions on the outsourced file.

Let us start with the global decoding algorithm. For the lifted RS code $\mathrm{Lift}_m(\mathrm{RS}_q[q, m])$, our global decoder works as follows. For each erasure, the decoding algorithm corrects it by finding, if it exists, a line going through the erasure and containing less than $d - 1$ other erasures (using interpolation as quoted in Sect. 5.1). If one or more erasures have been corrected during this step, the algorithm tries to correct the remaining erasures using the same method. Indeed, since some erasures were corrected, there exist lines with less erasures than before. If, during one iteration, no erasures have been corrected, the algorithm stops and returns the current vector. We give a pseudo-code description of this algorithm in Fig. 5.

Input: The encoded file V with potential erasures
Output: The encoded file $\tilde{F}$.
  repeat
    $E := \emptyset$
    for an erased position $x \in \mathbb{F}_q^m$
      if there exists a line $\ell \subseteq \mathbb{F}_q^m$ going through x with strictly less than d erasures.
        Use the global decoder of $\mathrm{RS}_q[q, d]$ on the restriction of the file to ℓ.
        We have corrected all the erasures on that line, x included.
        $E = E \cup \{x\}$
        Modify V accordingly.
  until $E = \emptyset$
  return V

Fig. 5. Our global decoding algorithm for lifted Reed-Solomon codes.

We now study the fail cases of the global decoding algorithm. Let $\mathrm{Lift}_m(\mathrm{RS}_q[q, d])$ be a lifted RS code. For an erased position $s \in \mathbb{F}_q^m$ to be unrecoverable, it is necessary that each line going through s possesses at least d erasures. However, it is not sufficient. Indeed, suppose that there exists a line ℓ going through s with exactly d erasures. If there exists an erasure position s' on the line ℓ and a line ℓ' going through s' with at most $d - 1$ erasures then the symbol erased at position s' can be recovered using the $\mathrm{RS}_q[q, d]$ decoder. Since s' lies on ℓ, this means that ℓ now contains only $d - 1$ erasures and they all can be corrected, the one at s included.

In order to capture a set of unrecoverable erasures for our global decoding algorithm, we introduce the following property:

Definition 5. *Let $\mathbb{F}_q$ be a finite field and m, d be positive integers. We say that a set $S \subseteq \mathbb{F}_q^m$ is a d-cover set if S verifies the following property:*

$$\forall s \in S, \forall \text{ line } \ell \subseteq \mathbb{F}_q^m \text{ going through } s, |S \cap \ell| \geq d$$

Or equivalently, for all line $\ell \subseteq \mathbb{F}_q^m, |S \cap \ell| = 0$ or $|S \cap \ell| \geq d$

Since the d-cover subsets of $\mathbb{F}_q^m$ represent the unrecoverable erasure patterns, we want to find an audit procedure that can detect their existence with high probability and low communication complexity. We propose the following audit:

1. The client randomly chooses a line $\ell \subseteq \mathbb{F}_q^m$.
2. The client retrieves the restriction of the outsourced file to the chosen line.
3. If it contains d or more erasures, reject, if not, accept.

The next step is to determine the probability that this audit detects a set of unrecoverable erasures if one exists. Let $S \subseteq \mathbb{F}_q^m$ be a non-empty d-cover set. Then there exists $s \in S$ and for each line ℓ going through s, $|\ell \cap S| \geq d$. We also know that for any line $\ell \subseteq \mathbb{F}_q^m$, either $|\ell \cap S| = 0$ or $|\ell \cap S| \geq d$.

Recall that $L := (q^m - 1)/(q - 1)$ is the number of lines going through a point in $\mathbb{F}_q^m$ and that $q^{m-1}L$ is the total number of lines in $\mathbb{F}_q^m$. Let ℓ be the randomly chosen line for the audit and s be an element of S. We have:

$$\Pr[|\ell \cap S| \neq 0] = \frac{L}{q^{m-1}L} + \left(1 - \frac{1}{q^{m-1}}\right) \cdot \Pr[|\ell \cap S| \neq 0 \mid s \notin \ell]$$

Let E be the event $\{|\ell \cap S| \neq 0 \mid s \notin \ell\}$. For each point $x \in \ell$, there is a unique line (xs) going through x and s. Since $s \in S$, this line contains at least d erased points in S, one being s. Since lines in $\mathbb{F}_q^m$ have q points, the probability that $x \in S$ is at least $(d-1)/(q-1)$. Moreover, if at least $q - d + 1$ points of ℓ do not belong to S we immediately know that $\ell \cap S = \emptyset$ since, by definition of S, either $|\ell \cap S| = 0$ or $|\ell \cap S| \geq d$. Thus, $\Pr[E] \geq 1 - (1 - (d-1)/(q-1))^{q-d+1}$.

Therefore, $\Pr[|\ell \cap S| \neq 0] \geq 1 - \left(1 - \frac{1}{q^{m-1}}\right)\left(1 - \frac{d-1}{q-1}\right)^{q-d+1}.$

The calculation we just made is essential. Indeed, since we supposed $S \neq \emptyset$, the event $\neg\{|\ell \cap S| \neq 0\}$ can be interpreted as 'on probed line ℓ, the audit accepts although the file is not retrievable'. In the CC security model for PoR, this is exactly the advantage of the distinguisher, *i.e.* the security of the scheme. In other words, we just upper-bounded the security of our PoR scheme.

We now formally prove the security of our PoR in the CC framework. We quickly describe the converters lift_rs_por$_{init}$ and lift_rs_por$_{audit}$. Both use the encoder and global decoder for lifted RS codes. On input $(\texttt{read}, i)$, both converters retrieve the whole memory using **read** requests, then they call the global decoder on the obtained word (corrupted values ϵ are replaced with erasures) and return the i-th symbol of the output if decoding succeeds. On input $(\texttt{write}, i, x)$, both converters retrieve the whole memory with read requests and decode it like before. If decoding succeeds, they replace the i-th symbol by x, encode the whole word and store it on the SMR using **write** requests.

On input **audit**, lift_rs_por$_{audit}$ chooses a random line $\ell \subseteq \mathbb{F}_q^m$ and retrieves the restriction of the outsourced file to ℓ through **read** requests. If the restriction contains d or more erasures, it returns **reject**. If not, it returns **accept**.

Theorem 1. *Let $d, m, \ell \in \mathbb{N}$, $\mathbb{F}_q$ be a finite field. The protocol* lift_rs_por $:=$ *(lift_rs_por$_{init}$, lift_rs_por$_{audit}$) for the lifted RS code* $\text{Lift}_m(\text{RS}_q[q,d])$ *of dimension ℓ constructs the auditable and authentic SMR, say* $\mathbf{aSMR}_{\Sigma,\ell}^{\text{audit}}$, *from* $\mathbf{aSMR}_{\Sigma,q^m}$, *with respect to the simulator* sim$_{audit}$. *More precisely, for all distinguishers* **D** *making at most r audits, we have*

$$\varDelta^{\mathbf{D}}(\text{lift\_rs\_por}_{\mathcal{P}}\, \mathbf{aSMR}_{\Sigma,q^m}, \text{sim}_{audit}^{\text{S}}\, \mathbf{aSMR}_{\Sigma,\ell}^{\text{audit}}) \leq r \cdot \left(1 - \frac{1}{q^{m-1}}\right)\left(1 - \frac{d-1}{q-1}\right)^{q-d+1}$$

Proof. Since our scheme is clearly correct (*i.e.* the client can always retrieve its file when there is no adversary), we alleviate notations and proofs by omitting correctness. We prove security by comparing the behaviors of the audit of the real system (the **aSMR** with the protocol) with that of the ideal one (the **aSMR**^{audit} with the simulator). We describe the simulator sim$_{auth}$. It maintains a simulated memory, emulating the real world memory, using the history of the ideal resource. On $(\texttt{delete}, i)$, the simulator replaces the i-th entry of its simulated memory by ϵ. On $(\texttt{restore}, i)$, the simulator restores the content of the i-th entry of its simulated memory to the last value written there. The simulator maintains a simulated history using the ideal history of the $\textbf{aSMR}^{\textsf{audit}}$.

If, after a $\texttt{delete}$ request, the set of corrupted locations of the simulated memory contains a d-cover subset of $\mathbb{F}_q^m$, the simulator deletes the whole ideal memory by sending $\texttt{delete}$ requests to $\textbf{aSMR}^{\textsf{audit}}$. Similarly, if after a $\texttt{restore}$ request, the set of corrupted locations of the simulated memory does not contain a d-cover subset of $\mathbb{F}_q^m$, the simulator restores the whole ideal memory by sending $\texttt{restore}$ requests to $\textbf{aSMR}^{\textsf{audit}}$.

On an $\texttt{audit}$ request, the simulator chooses a random line $\ell \subseteq \mathbb{F}_q^m$, adds the entries $(\texttt{read}, i)$ for $i \in \ell$ to its simulated history. Then, if the restriction of its simulated memory to ℓ contains strictly less than d corrupted cells, the simulator sends $\texttt{allow}$ to $\textbf{aSMR}^{\textsf{audit}}$. Else, it instructs the $\textbf{aSMR}^{\textsf{audit}}$ to output $\texttt{reject}$.

Upon $\texttt{auditReq}$ at Interface $\textsf{S}_H$: Recall that d-cover sets are the sets of unrecoverable erasures for our global decoder of lifted RS codes. Suppose that a subset of the corrupted cells forms a d-cover set. In order to run the audit, the converter chooses a random line $\ell \subseteq \mathbb{F}_q^m$, retrieves the restriction of the memory to this line through $\texttt{read}$ requests and adds the corresponding entries to its simulated history. We showed, see Eq. 5.2, that the probability that this restriction contains strictly less than d erasures, *i.e.*, that the audit is successful, is less than $(1 - 1/q^{m-1})(1 - (d-1)/(q-1))^{q-d+1}$.

The simulation is perfect unless the following BAD event occurs: *having simulated a real audit, the simulator answers $\texttt{allow}$ (audit should succeed) whereas a d-cover subset of corrupted cells exists.* In that case, the simulator has chosen a restriction of the memory to a line ℓ that contains strictly less than d corrupted cells, and has written the corresponding $\texttt{read}$ requests to its simulated history. Note that the distinguisher has access to the simulated history. Then, the simulator outputs $\texttt{allow}$ to the ideal resource, that runs the ideal audit. Since there exists a d-cover set of corrupted memory cells, the file is unretrievable so the ideal audit fails and the client receives $\texttt{reject}$. The distinguisher thus observes the following incoherence: $\texttt{reject}$ is output while the (simulated) history contains the trace of a valid audit. The adversary knows that this is the ideal system.

To sum up, the only observable difference from a distinguisher point of view lies in the audit procedure. The overall distinguishing probability is thus the one of distinguishing a real audit from a simulated one. As we saw, if the distinguisher runs r audits, this probability is less than $r \cdot (1 - 1/q^{m-1}) \cdot (1 - (d-1)/(q-1))^{q-d+1}$, yielding the aforementioned result. □

5.3 The Graph Code PoR Scheme

We give another instantiation of our framework using the graph codes of Tanner [16]. We briefly recall how these codes are constructed.

Let $G = (V, E)$ be a q-regular graph on n vertices. For a vertex $v \in V$, let $\Gamma(v)$ be the set of vertices adjacent to v. Let $\mathbb{F}$ be a finite field and let $\mathcal{C}_0 \subseteq \mathbb{F}^q$ be a linear code, called the *inner* code. Fix an arbitrary order on the edges incident to each vertex of G and let $\Gamma_i(v)$ be the i-th neighbor of v. A Tanner code is defined as the set of all labelings of the edges of G that respect the inner code $\mathcal{C}_0$. Formally,

Definition 6 (Tanner code). *Let $G = (V, E)$ be a q-regular graph on n vertices and let $\mathcal{C}_0 \subseteq \mathbb{F}^q$ be a linear code. The Tanner code $\mathcal{C}(G, \mathcal{C}_0) \subseteq \mathbb{F}^E$ is a linear code of length $nq/2$, so that for $c \in \mathbb{F}^E$, $c \in \mathcal{C}(G, \mathcal{C}_0)$ if and only if, for all $v \in V$, $(c_{(v, \Gamma_1(v))}, \ldots, c_{(v, \Gamma_q(v))}) \in \mathcal{C}_0$.*

One can easily check, by counting constraints, that if $\mathcal{C}_0$ has rate R, then $\mathcal{C}(G, \mathcal{C}_0)$ has rate at least $2R-1$. These codes possess some sort of local correction. Indeed, to correct an edge e incident to a vertex v, one can retrieve the vector $(c_{(v, \Gamma_1(v))}, \ldots, c_{(v, \Gamma_q(v))})$ of labels of edges incident to v and correct it using the decoder of $\mathcal{C}_0$.

In the following, let d be the minimum distance of the inner code. Again, using the composability of CC, we only have to deal with potential erasures. Following our framework of Sect. 3, we start by sketching our global decoder. In the following, we say that an edge is *erased* when the label of that edge is erased. Similarly, we say that we *correct* an edge if we correct the label of that edge.

Assume that we want to correct an erasure on an edge e incident to a vertex v. If v is incident to less than $d-1$ erased edges, we can use the erasure decoding of $\mathcal{C}_0$ to correct all the edges incident to v, e included. Otherwise, v is incident to $k > d-1$ erased edges. Pick an erased edge incident to v. This edge is also incident to a vertex $v' \neq v$. If v' is incident to less than $d-1$ erased edges, we can correct them all and v is now incident to $k-1$ erased edges. If $k-1 \leq d-1$ we can correct the edge e. Else, we iterate the process on v and its neighbors.

Now, we have to characterize the configurations of erased edges that are unrecoverable for our decoding algorithm. We claim that these unrecoverable configurations correspond to subgraphs of G of minimum degree d. Indeed, these are the graph analogues of the d-cover sets for lifted RS codes. We prove our claim: suppose that the subgraph formed by the unrecoverable edges possesses a vertex v incident to less than $d-1$ unrecoverable edges. Then, by iterating the local decoding algorithm, we can recover the other edges incident to v so that only these unrecoverable edges remain erased. Then, since there are less than $d-1$ erased edges incident to v and since the minimum distance of the inner code is d, we can correct all the edges incident to v using the decoder of the inner code. This is in contradiction with these edges being unrecoverable.

Finally, the audit consists in randomly choosing a vertex v and retrieving the vector $w := (c_{(v, \Gamma_1(v))}, \ldots, c_{(v, \Gamma_q(v))})$ of labeling of edges incident to v. If w contains d or more erasures, the audit rejects. Else, it accepts.

The security of the audit depends on the graph G and the minimum distance d of the inner code $\mathcal{C}_0$. The bigger the minimum subgraphs of G with minimum degree d are, the better the security of the PoR will be. Indeed, let s be the minimum size (number of vertices) of a subgraph of G with minimum degree d. For a configuration of unrecoverable erasures to exist, we thus need at least s

vertices of G with at least d erased edges. Recall that our audit chooses a random vertex of G and accepts if and only if this vertex is incident to less than $d-1$ erased edges. Thus, the probability that our audit accepts when there exists an unrecoverable set of erased edges is less than $1 - s/|V|$. In our framework, this is exactly the advantage of the adversary in breaking the security of our PoR. A similar proof ans simulator to the ones of Theorem 1 yield the following theorem:

Theorem 2. *Let $G = (V, E)$ be a q-regular graph with $|V| = n$ and let $\mathcal{C}_0 \subseteq \mathbb{F}^q$ be a linear code with minimum distance d and rate R. Let s be the minimum size (number of vertices) of a subgraph of G with minimum degree d. The protocol $\mathsf{graph\_por} := (\mathsf{graph\_por}_{\mathsf{init}}, \mathsf{graph\_por}_{\mathsf{audit}})$ for a Tanner code $\mathcal{C}(G, \mathcal{C}_0)$ of length $nq/2$ and rate at least $2R - 1$ that:*

1. *Starts by encoding the file and uploads it to the server.*
2. *On an* audit *request, chooses a random vertex $v \in V$ and accepts if and only if v is incident to less than $d-1$ erased edges.*
3. *Extracts the file using the algorithm sketched above.*

constructs the auditable and authentic SMR, say $\mathsf{aSMR}^{\mathsf{audit}}_{\mathbb{F},(2R-1)nq/2}$, from $\mathsf{aSMR}_{\mathbb{F},nq/2}$, with respect to the simulator $\mathsf{sim}_{\mathsf{audit}}$. More precisely, for all distinguishers $\mathbf{D}$ making at most r audits, we have

$$\Delta^{\mathbf{D}}(\mathsf{graph\_por}_{\mathcal{P}} \, \mathsf{aSMR}_{\mathbb{F},nq/2}, \mathsf{sim}^{\mathsf{S}}_{\mathsf{audit}} \, \mathsf{aSMR}^{\mathsf{audit}}_{\mathbb{F},(2R-1)nq/2}) \leq r \cdot \left(1 - \frac{s}{n}\right)$$

6   Parameters

The impact of the choice of the lifted RS code on the parameters of our lifted RS PoR scheme are highlighted in Fig. 7. The grey line gives a choice of parameters with a storage overhead of 13.9% and total communication of 0.01% of the file size. Increasing the length q of the RS base code decreases the storage overhead and increasing the lifting parameter m increases the size of the file stored. Exact formulae for the parameters of our scheme is given in Fig. 6.

Let us compare our parameters with the ones of [11]. First, in both schemes, the client's file is encoded using a lifted RS code and the audit consists in probing the restriction of this codeword to a random affine line. In our case, we authenticate the data using our MAC based authentication protocol (see Sect. 4) whereas [11] binds data to a specific location by using an encryption scheme. Let κ be the computational security parameter of both schemes and Σ be the alphabet of the code. Our scheme stores a code symbol along with a MAC tag, that is $\kappa + \log|\Sigma|$ bits, in each memory location of the server whereas [11] stores a ciphertext, that is κ bits, in each memory location. Since $\log|\Sigma| \ll \kappa$ (we have $\kappa = 128$ and $|\Sigma| = q$ in Fig. 7), our scheme and the one of [11] have very close storage overhead and communication complexity. In [11], the minimum distance of the code d is chosen to be equal to 2. Using our security analysis of Theorem 1, we show that the [11] scheme has only 1.44 bits of statistical security, when $d = 2$, whereas state-of-the-art schemes expect at least 40. See Fig. 7 for our recommended parameters.

A major benefit of our scheme is that our audit produces less "false positives" than the one of [11]. For PoRs, a false positive occurs when an audit rejects while the file is still retrievable. In other words, the client thinks that he lost his file, but it is still retrievable in full. The number of false positive audits has no influence on the security of the PoR but, in practice, it is a situation that we absolutely wish to avoid. The audit of [11] rejects if the restriction of the file to an affine line does not belong to the RS base code. In other words, if there is at least one corruption on the line probed by the audit, it deems the file unretrievable. If the adversary introduces at least one erasure on every line of the space, the audit would always reject independently of the correction capability (*i.e.* the minimum distance) of the code. Using our framework and our authentication protocol, we are able to fix this problem. Indeed, our audit deems the file unretrievable only if the probed line contains at least d erasures, where d is the minimum distance of the RS base code. This means that we drastically decrease the number of false positive audits, making our scheme much more reliable and usable in practice.

For example, suppose that the outsourced file is encoded using a lifted RS code over $\mathbb{F}_q^2$ with minimum distance $d \geq 3$. Let ℓ_1, ℓ_2 be two intersecting lines in $\mathbb{F}_q^2$. Suppose that an adversary erases all the file's symbols at the locations given by ℓ_1 and ℓ_2 and no other symbols. Of course, the file is still retrievable since the local decoder can correct all the erasures of $\ell_1 \setminus \ell_2$ by querying all the lines parallel to ℓ_2 (these lines contain only one erasure and $d \geq 3$). Then, the local decoder can correct all the erasures of ℓ_2 by querying any line intersecting ℓ_2. Unfortunately, in this situation, the audit of [11] rejects with probability 1. Indeed, their audit chooses a random line ℓ in $\mathbb{F}_q^2$ and rejects if ℓ contains at least one erasure. This is always the case here since, either ℓ intersects ℓ_1 or, ℓ is parallel to ℓ_1 and is thus intersecting ℓ_2. This is not the case with our audit. Indeed, since only two lines of $\mathbb{F}_q^2$ have d or more erasures, our audit rejects with probability $2/(q^2 + q)$ since there are $q^2 + q$ lines in $\mathbb{F}_q^2$.

Future work includes evaluating the efficiency of our Tanner code PoRs according to different choices of inner codes and graphs as well as instantiating our framework with other families of high-rate locally correctable codes.

	Exact value	Asymptotics
C. storage overhead	κ	$\mathcal{O}(1)$
S. storage overhead	$(\frac{1}{R} - 1)\lvert F\rvert + q^m\kappa$	$\mathcal{O}(\lvert F\rvert)$
C. $\to$ S.	$2m\log q$	$\mathcal{O}(\lvert F\rvert)$
S. $\to$ C.	$q(\kappa + \log q)$	$\mathcal{O}(\lvert F\rvert^{1/m})$

Fig. 6. The exact parameters of our scheme. $\lvert F\rvert$ denotes the file size in bits, κ the security parameter of the MAC, q the field size and $m \geq 2$ the lifting parameter. We have $Rq^m \log q = \lvert F\rvert$.

PoR param.			Results					
m	q	d	$\|F\|$ (bits)	$\frac{1}{R}-1$	comm. C. → S. (bits)	comm. S. → C. (bits)	comm./$\|F\|$	Statistical Security
2	256	32	255003	1.056	32	2048	0.0081	2^{-42}
	512		1446533	0.631	36	4608	0.0032	2^{-43}
	1024		7441987	0.409	40	10240	0.0013	2^{-44}
	2048		36072982	0.279	44	22528	0.0006	2^{-44}
	4096		168474135	0.195	48	49152	0.0003	2^{-44}
	8192		765948403	0.139	52	106496	0.0001	2^{-44}
	1024	64	6389859	0.641	40	10240	0.0016	2^{-88}
	2048		32605896	0.415	44	22528	0.0007	2^{-89}
	4096		157041023	0.282	48	49152	0.0003	2^{-90}
	8192		728834780	0.197	52	106496	0.0001	2^{-90}

Fig. 7. Different choices of lifted Reed-Solomon codes for our PoR scheme.

References

1. Badertscher, C., Maurer, U.: Composable and robust outsourced storage. In: Smart, N.P. (ed.) CT-RSA 2018. LNCS, vol. 10808, pp. 354–373. Springer, Cham (2018). https://doi.org/10.1007/978-3-319-76953-0_19

2. Bowers, K.D., Juels, A., Oprea, A.: Proofs of retrievability: theory and implementation. In: Proceedings of the 2009 ACM Workshop on Cloud Computing Security, CCSW 2009, New York, NY, USA, pp. 43–54. ACM (2009). https://doi.org/10.1145/1655008.1655015

3. Canetti, R.: Universally composable security: a new paradigm for cryptographic protocols. In: Proceedings 42nd IEEE Symposium on Foundations of Computer Science (2001). https://doi.org/10.1109/sfcs.2001.959888

4. Dodis, Y., Vadhan, S., Wichs, D.: Proofs of retrievability via hardness amplification. In: Reingold, O. (ed.) TCC 2009. LNCS, vol. 5444, pp. 109–127. Springer, Heidelberg (2009). https://doi.org/10.1007/978-3-642-00457-5_8

5. Guo, A., Kopparty, S., Sudan, M.: New affine-invariant codes from lifting. In: Proceedings of the 4th Conference on Innovations in Theoretical Computer Science, ITCS 2013, New York, NY, USA, pp. 529–540. ACM (2013). https://doi.org/10.1145/2422436.2422494

6. Hemenway, B., Ostrovsky, R., Wootters, M.: Local correctability of expander codes. In: Fomin, F.V., Freivalds, R., Kwiatkowska, M., Peleg, D. (eds.) ICALP 2013. LNCS, vol. 7965, pp. 540–551. Springer, Heidelberg (2013). https://doi.org/10.1007/978-3-642-39206-1_46

7. Jost, D., Maurer, U.: Overcoming impossibility results in composable security using interval-wise guarantees. In: Micciancio, D., Ristenpart, T. (eds.) CRYPTO 2020. LNCS, vol. 12170, pp. 33–62. Springer, Cham (2020). https://doi.org/10.1007/978-3-030-56784-2_2

8. Juels, A., Kaliski, B.S., Jr.: PORs: proofs of retrievability for large files. In: Proceedings of the 14th ACM Conference on Computer and Communications Security, CCS 2007, New York, NY, USA, pp. 584–597. ACM (2007). https://doi.org/10.1145/1315245.1315317

9. Katz, J., Trevisan, L.: On the efficiency of local decoding procedures for error-correcting codes. In: Proceedings of the Thirty-Second Annual ACM Symposium

on Theory of Computing, STOC 2000, New York, NY, USA, pp. 80–86. ACM (2000). https://doi.org/10.1145/335305.335315

10. Kopparty, S., Saraf, S., Yekhanin, S.: High-rate codes with sublinear-time decoding. In: Proceedings of the Forty-Third Annual ACM Symposium on Theory of Computing, STOC 2011, New York, NY, USA, pp. 167–176. ACM (2011). https://doi.org/10.1145/1993636.1993660

11. Lavauzelle, J., Levy-Dit-Vehel, F.: New proofs of retrievability using locally decodable codes. In: International Symposium on Information Theory ISIT 2016, Barcelona, Spain, pp. 1809–1813 (2016). https://doi.org/10.1109/ISIT.2016.7541611

12. Maurer, U.: Constructive cryptography – a new paradigm for security definitions and proofs. In: Mödersheim, S., Palamidessi, C. (eds.) TOSCA 2011. LNCS, vol. 6993, pp. 33–56. Springer, Heidelberg (2012). https://doi.org/10.1007/978-3-642-27375-9_3

13. Maurer, U., Renner, R.: Abstract cryptography. In: Innovations in Computer Science. Tsinghua University Press (2011)

14. Paterson, M., Stinson, D., Upadhyay, J.: A coding theory foundation for the analysis of general unconditionally secure proof-of-retrievability schemes for cloud storage. J. Math. Cryptol. **7**(3), 183–216 (2013). https://doi.org/10.1515/jmc-2013-5002

15. Shacham, H., Waters, B.: Compact proofs of retrievability. In: Pieprzyk, J. (ed.) ASIACRYPT 2008. LNCS, vol. 5350, pp. 90–107. Springer, Heidelberg (2008). https://doi.org/10.1007/978-3-540-89255-7_7

16. Tanner, R.: A recursive approach to low complexity codes. IEEE Trans. Inf. Theory **27**(5), 533–547 (1981). https://doi.org/10.1109/TIT.1981.1056404

Compression Point in Field
of Characteristic 3

Ismail Assoujaa$^{(\boxtimes)}$ (iD), Siham Ezzouak$^{(\boxtimes)}$, and Hakima Mouanis

University Sidi Mohammed Ben Abdellah FSDM (labo: LASMA), Fez, Morocco
{ismail.assoujja,siham.ezzouak}@usmba.ac.ma

Abstract. For some applications, systems and devices, it might be desirable to take as few as possible of bit memory space and still keep the same result. Compression point is a new method that used some arithmetic operation in (ECC) elliptic curve cryptography to reduce memory space. If we take any point on the elliptic curve, we can see that this point is consisting of two coordinates x and y, so with compression point we can compressed this point and keep only one coordinate x or y and one sign bit/trit, requiring only half the space. In this paper, we will show new methods of compression point that can save 25% of the space memory in fields of characteristic 3, and compare it with previous result.

Keywords: Elliptic curve · Compression point · Affine coordinate · Field of characteristic 3

1   Introduction

The benefice of (ECC), which was finded by the authers of [1,2] independently (Neal Koblitz and Victor Miller) is that requires a smaller key sizes (less memory space) than the other public cryptosystems. Compression point method is used if we want to compress the points on the elliptic curve which contain two coordinates x and y, to reduce them into just one coordinate x or y and one sign bit/trit, this compression can save half of the memory space but add a numbers of arithmetic operation like inversion, square, multiplication, square root and cube root operation, the last two operations are hard to calculate. In general and also in [4], an elliptic curve is define as $P(x,y) = f(x) - y^2 = x^3 + ax^2 + b - y^2 = 0$, a point (x,y) on this curve $E(\mathbb{F}_{q^3})$ is compressed as (x,β) where β is a single sign bit, to return to the full point (x,y), we can decompress the value y are recovered it from (x,β) by solving for y the curve equation $P(x,y) = 0$, which involves computing a square root $\sqrt{f(x)}$. There is other way to apply compression point, it when compress (x,y) as (α,y), to return to the full point (x,y) we can recover the point x by solving the curve equation for x instead of y, in this case a cubic root is required. In the 21th centuries, a lot of researchers was developing more and more application in this fields [6–11]. Khabbazian et al. in [5] have remarked that two points $P_1 = (x_1,y_1)$ and $P_2 = (x_2,y_2)$ may be simultaneously compressed as $(x_1, x_2, y_1 + y_2)$, thus we take the addition of the

A. Nitaj and K. Zkik (Eds.): I4CS 2022, CCIS 1747, pp. 104–111, 2022.
https://doi.org/10.1007/978-3-031-23201-5_7

two y-coordinates and combined them into one. Also we can compress two points $P_1 = (x_1; y_1)$ and $P_2 = (x_2; y_2)$ as $(x_1 + x_2, y_1, y_2)$ and when we work with this method we can save 25% of the memory space. The present article extended the previous results in a field of characteristic 3. More precisely, we will compare our work with the basic arithmetic operation of elliptic curves in a field of characteristic 3 with affine coordinate. The article is organized as follows: so in Sect. 2, we recall some background on the basics arithmetic operation of elliptic curves in a field of characteristic 3 with affine coordinate. Section 3 presents our main theorems in this work and the results of our work. Eventually, Sect. 4 concludes the paper and provides some perspectives for further works.

2   Mathematical Background

In everything that follows, we shall use, without explicit mention, the following:

- **p**: prime number.
- **q**: power of prime number.
- **E**: An elliptic curve over the field $\mathbb{F}_q$.
- **P$_\infty$**: point a l'infinity.
- $\mathbf{E[r]} = \{P \in E(\mathbb{F}_p) \backslash [r]P = P_\infty\}$.
- $\mathbf{E(\mathbb{F}_q)}$: Set of all points on elliptic curve E defined over $\mathbb{F}_q$ and including P_∞.
- $\#\mathbf{E(\mathbb{F}_q)}$: Number of points on the curve, called also the order of the curve E.
- $\mathbb{F}_q$: The finite field containing q elements. For this Standard, q shall be a power of 3 ($q = 3^m$).
- I: inversion. • M: multiplication. • S: squaring.
- SR: square root. • CR: cube root.

2.1   Arithmetic of Elliptic Curve with Affine Coordinate in a Field of Characteristic 3

(see [6] 3–4) In characteristic 3, every ordinary elliptic curve over the finite field $\mathbb{F}_{3^m}$ can be written in the Weierstrass form:

$$y^2 = x^3 + ax^2 + b, \text{ where } a, b \in \mathbb{F}_{3^m} \text{ and } ab \neq 0.$$

- **Addition:**
  The addition of two (different) points $(x_1, y_1), (x_2, y_2)$ on E is the point (x_3, y_3) given by

Operation	Formula	with
Addition (1)	$x_3 = \lambda^2 - x_1 - x_2 - a$	$\lambda = \frac{(y_2 - y_1)}{(x_2 - x_1)}$
	$y_3 = \lambda(x_1 - x_3) - y_1$	

The cost of the addition formulas are I + 2M + S.

3   Compression Point

To work with this new methods of compression point, we will follow the steps bellow:

1. Take the elliptic curve equation in the field of characteristic 3 with affine coordinate.
2. Instead of take the values of $P = (x_1, y_1), Q = (x_2, y_2)$ we keep only the value of $(x_1, x_2, \alpha = y_1 + y_2)$ or $(\alpha = x_1 + x_2, y_1, y_2)$.
3. Calculate the value of $\beta = y_1 - y_2$ or $\beta = x_1 - x_2$.
4. Calculate the cost of decompression.
5. Replace the value of y_1, y_2 or x_1, x_2 in the formula of addition.
6. Calculate the cost of the new addition, for the cost of new addition is require the cost of decompressions plus the cost of classical addition.

3.1   First Wew Compression Points

In field of characteristic 3, the elliptic curve equation E with affine coordinate is given by:
$$y^2 = f(x) = x^3 + ax^2 + b.$$

Instead of take the values of $P = (x_1, y_1), Q = (x_2, y_2)$ such that $P \neq \pm Q$, we take the value of $(x_1, x_2, \alpha = y_1 + y_2)$.

• If $a = 0$, we have $y^2 = f(x) = x^3 + b$. (a cuspidal cubic or semi cubical parabola curve)

We can calculate

$$\beta = y_1 - y_2 = \frac{(y_1 - y_2)(y_1 + y_2)}{y_1 + y_2} = \frac{y_1^2 - y_2^2}{y_1 + y_2} = \frac{f(x_1) - f(x_2)}{\alpha} = \frac{x_1^3 - x_2^3}{\alpha}$$

so $y_1 = \frac{\alpha + \beta}{2}$ and $y_2 = \frac{\alpha - \beta}{2}$
To compute β, we need $2C + I = 2S + 2M + I$.

Algorithm 1. y-coordinate decompression with affine coordinate with a=0

    Input: $(x_1, x_2, \alpha = y_1 + y_2)$
    Output: (y_1, y_2)

1: $\beta \leftarrow y_1 - y_2 = \frac{x_1^3 - x_2^3}{\alpha}$
2: $y_1 \leftarrow \frac{\alpha + \beta}{2}$
3: $y_2 \leftarrow \frac{\alpha - \beta}{2}$
4: return (y_1, y_2)

Addition:
We take $(x_1, x_2, \alpha = y_1 + y_2)$ to calculate the addition $P \oplus Q = (x_3, y_3)$
We replace the value of y_1 and y_2 in the formulas (1) of classical addition above.
So the new formulas of addition become:

Operation	Formula	with
Addition	$x_3 = \lambda^2 - x_1 - x_2$	$\beta = \frac{x_1^3 - x_2^3}{\alpha}$
	$y_3 = (x_1 - x_3)\lambda - \frac{\alpha+\beta}{2}$	$\lambda = \frac{\beta}{x_1 - x_2}$

The cost of this addition formulas require $2I + 4M + 3S$.

- If $a \neq 0$,

We can calculate

$$\beta = y_1 - y_2 = \frac{(y_1 - y_2)(y_1 + y_2)}{y_1 + y_2} = \frac{y_1^2 - y_2^2}{y_1 + y_2} = \frac{f(x_1) - f(x_2)}{\alpha} = \frac{x_1^3 + ax_1^2 - x_2^3 - ax_2^2}{\alpha}$$

so $y_1 = \frac{\alpha+\beta}{2}$ and $y_2 = \frac{\alpha-\beta}{2}$
To compute β, we need $2C + I = 2M + 2S + I$.

Algorithm 2. y-coordinate decompression with affine coordinate with $a \neq 0$

   Input: $(x_1, x_2, \alpha = y_1 + y_2)$
   Output: (y_1, y_2)
1: $\beta \leftarrow y_1 - y_2 = \frac{x_1^3 - x_2^3 + a(x_1^2 - x_2^2)}{\alpha}$
2: $y_1 \leftarrow \frac{\alpha+\beta}{2}$
3: $y_2 \leftarrow \frac{\alpha-\beta}{2}$
4: return (y_1, y_2)

Addition:
We take $(x_1, x_2, \alpha = y_1 + y_2)$ to calculate the addition $P \oplus Q = (x_3, y_3)$
We replace the value of y_1 and y_2 in the formulas (1) of classical addition above.
So the new formulas of addition become:
   The cost of this addition formulas require $2I + 4M + 3S$.

Operation	Formula	with
Addition	$x_3 = \lambda^2 - x_1 - x_2 - a$	$\beta = \frac{x_1^3 - x_2^3 + a(x_1^2 - x_2^2)}{\alpha}$
	$y_3 = \lambda(x_1 - x_3) - \frac{\alpha+\beta}{2}$	$\lambda = \frac{\beta}{x_1 - x_2}$

3.2 The Second New Compression Points to Reduce Memory

In field of characteristic 3, the elliptic curve equation E with affine coordinate is given by:

$$y^2 = f(x) = x^3 + ax^2 + b.$$

Instead of take the values of $P = (x_1, y_1)$ and $Q = (x_2, y_2)$ such that $P \neq \pm Q$ we take the value of $(\alpha = x_1 + x_2, y_1, y_2)$.

- If $a = 0$ we have $y^2 = f(x) = x^3 + b$.

We compute

$$\beta = x_1 - x_2 = \sqrt[3]{(x_1 - x_2)^3} = \sqrt[3]{x_1^3 - x_2^3} = \sqrt[3]{y_1^2 - y_2^2}$$

because $3x_1x_2^3 = 0 = 3x_1^2x_2 \ (char(\mathbb{F}_q) = 3)$,
so $x_1 = \frac{\alpha+\beta}{2}$ and $x_2 = \frac{\alpha-\beta}{2}$
To compute β we need 1CR + 2S.

Algorithm 3. x-coordinate decompression with affine coordinate with a=0

    Input: $(\alpha = x_1 + x_2, y_1, y_2)$
    Output: (x_1, x_2)
1: $\beta \leftarrow x_1 - x_2 = \sqrt[3]{y_1^2 - y_2^2}$
2: $x_1 \leftarrow \frac{\alpha+\beta}{2}$
3: $x_2 \leftarrow \frac{\alpha-\beta}{2}$
4: return (x_1, x_2)

Addition:
We take $(\alpha = x_1 + x_2, y_1, y_2)$ to calculate the addition $P \oplus Q = (x_3, y_3)$
We replace the value of x_1 and x_2 in the formulas (1) of classical addition above.
So the new formulas of addition become:

Operation	Formula	with
Addition	$x_3 = \lambda^2 - \alpha$	$\beta = \sqrt[3]{y_1^2 - y_2^2}$
	$y_3 = \lambda(\frac{\alpha+\beta}{2} - x_3) - y_1$	$\lambda = \frac{y_1 - y_2}{\beta}$

The cost of this addition formulas require 1I + 2M + 3S + 1CR.

- If $a \neq 0$

We have $y_1^2 - y_2^2 = x_1^3 + ax_1^2 - x_2^3 - ax_2^2$,
$y_1^2 - y_2^2 = x_1^3 - x_2^3 + ax_1^2 - ax_2^2$
$y_1^2 - y_2^2 = (x_1 - x_2)^3 + a(x_1 + x_2)(x_1 - x_2)$.
We can calculate $\beta = x_1 - x_2$ by resolving the cubic equation:

$$\beta^3 + a\alpha\beta = y_1^2 - y_2^2$$

So the solution of this cubic equation is given by:

$$\beta = \sqrt[3]{\frac{y_1^2 - y_2^2}{2} + \sqrt{\frac{(y_1^2 - y_2^2)^2}{4} + \frac{(a\alpha)^3}{27}}} + \sqrt[3]{\frac{y_1^2 - y_2^2}{2} - \sqrt{\frac{(y_1^2 - y_2^2)^2}{4} + \frac{(a\alpha)^3}{27}}}$$

Algorithm 4. x-coordinate decompression with affine coordinate with $a \neq 0$

    Input: $(\alpha = x_1 + x_2, y_1, y_2)$
    Output: (x_1, x_2)

1: $\beta \leftarrow x_1 - x_2 = \sqrt[3]{\frac{y_1^2 - y_2^2}{2} + \sqrt{\frac{(y_1^2 - y_2^2)^2}{4} + \frac{(a\alpha)^3}{27}}} + \sqrt[3]{\frac{y_1^2 - y_2^2}{2} - \sqrt{\frac{(y_1^2 - y_2^2)^2}{4} + \frac{(a\alpha)^3}{27}}}$

2: $x_1 \leftarrow \frac{\alpha + \beta}{2}$

3: $x_2 \leftarrow \frac{\alpha - \beta}{2}$

4: return (x_1, x_2)

---

so $x_1 = \frac{\alpha + \beta}{2}$ and $x_2 = \frac{\alpha - \beta}{2}$

To compute β, we need 2CR + 1SR + C + 3S = 2CR + 1SR + 4S + M.

Addition:

We take $(\alpha = x_1 + x_2, y_1, y_2)$ to calculate the addition $P \oplus Q = (x_3, y_3)$

We replace the value of x_1 and x_2 in the formulas (1) of classical addition above. So the new formulas of addition become:

Operation	Formula	with
Addition	$x_3 = \lambda^2 - \alpha - a$	$\beta = \sqrt[3]{\frac{y_1^2 - y_2^2}{2} + \sqrt{\frac{(y_1^2 - y_2^2)^2}{4} + \frac{(a\alpha)^3}{27}}} + \sqrt[3]{\frac{y_1^2 - y_2^2}{2} - \sqrt{\frac{(y_1^2 - y_2^2)^2}{4} + \frac{(a\alpha)^3}{27}}}$
	$y_3 = \lambda(\frac{\alpha + \beta}{2} - x_3) - y_1$	$\lambda = \frac{y_1 - y_2}{\beta}$

The cost of this addition formulas require 1I + 3M + 5S + 1SR + 2CR.

3.3 Comparison

For all these compression points, we can save at least 25% of memory size, also, we don't need any operation to calculate the compression, so the table below show their cost (Table 1):

Table 1. The cost of decompression and addition

Operation of addition	Decompression cost	Addition cost
No compression:	0	1I+2M+ S
Compression with $(x_1; x_2; \alpha = y_1 + y_2)$ if a=0	1I+2M+2S	2I+4M+3S
Compression with $(x_1; x_2; \alpha = y_1 + y_2)$ if $a \neq 0$	1I+2M+2S	2I+4M+3S
Compression with $(\alpha = x_1 + x_2; y_1; y_2)$ if a=0	2S+1CR	1I+2M+3S+1CR
Compression with $(\alpha = x_1 + x_2; y_1; y_2)$ if $a \neq 0$	M+4S+1SR+2CR	1I+3M+5S+1SR+2CR

In the table above we see that the cost of new addition in affine coordinate is the cost of classical addition I+2M+S plus the cost of decompression to save 25% of memory.

- So, in the case of compression with $(x_1; x_2; \alpha = y_1 + y_2)$ the cost of decompression is I + 2M + 2S, so the cost of new addition is 2I + 4M + 4S.

- Also, in the case of compression with $(\alpha = x_1 + x_2; y_1; y_2)$ if $a = 0$, the cost of decompression is 1CR + 2S, so the cost of new addition is 1I + 1CR + 2M + 3S.
- Finally, in the case of compression with $(\alpha = x_1 + x_2; y_1; y_2)$ if $a \neq 0$, the cost of decompression is 2CR + 1SR + 4S + M, so the cost of new addition is 2CR + 1SR + 5S + 3M + 1I.

The complexity of Addition:
Cipolla's in [4], show that the complexity of square-root algorithm attains $O(m^3 log^3 q)$ for any finite field $\mathbb{F}_{q^m}$, particularly he give an efficient algorithm to compute r-th roots in $\mathbb{F}_{q^m}$ with complexity $O((logm + rlogq)m^2 log^2 q)$ so for compute the cube root we have a complexity of $O((logm + 3logq)m^2 log^2 q)$. In [3], to compute multiplication, we have a complexity of $O(mlogm)$ and to compute inversion we have a complexity of $O(mlog^2 mloglogm)$. For this study, we work with field of characteristic 3, so $\mathbb{F}_{q^m} = \mathbb{F}_{3^m}$ thus $q = 3$ (Table 2). So $M = O(mlogm)$, $I = O(mlog^2 mloglogm)$, $SR = O(logm + 2log3)m^2 log^2 3)$ and $CR = O((logm + 3log3)m^2 log^2 3)$, our table above in term of complicity become

Table 2. The complexity of addition

Operation of addition	Addition complexity
No compression:	$O(mlogm(3+logmloglogm))$
Compression with $(x_1; x_2; \alpha = y_1 + y_2)$ if a=0	$O(mlogm(7+2logmloglogm))$
Compression with $(x_1; x_2; \alpha = y_1 + y_2)$ if $a \neq 0$	$O(mlogm(7+2logmloglogm))$
Compression with $(\alpha = x_1 + x_2; y_1; y_2)$ if a=0	$O(mlogm(5 + mlog^2 3 + logmloglogm))$
Compression with $(\alpha = x_1 + x_2; y_1; y_2)$ if $a \neq 0$	$O(mlogm(8 + 3mlog^2 3 + logmloglogm)) + 8m^2 log^3 3$

4   Conclusions

In this work, we provided details and important improvements of two new methods of compression points in a field of characteristic 3 with two type of curve $y^2 = x^3 + b$ and $y^2 = x^3 + ax^2 + b$, also provide the cost of these operations and complexity. We see that if our method of $(x_1, x_2, \alpha = y_1 + y_2)$ costs the same complexity time, our method can achieve better implementation efficiency compared with the classical method, so it will save 25% of memory size. Moreover, we see that we work with this compression point $(x_1, x_2, \alpha = y_1 + y_2)$ is more better than the other compression point $(\alpha = x_1 + x_2, y_1, y_2)$.

References

1. Koblitz, N.: Elliptic curve cryptosystems. Math. Comput. **48**, 203–209 (1987)
2. Miller, V.S.: Use of elliptic curves in cryptography. In: Williams, H.C. (ed.) CRYPTO 1985. LNCS, vol. 218, pp. 417–426. Springer, Heidelberg (1986). https://doi.org/10.1007/3-540-39799-X_31

3. Gashkov, S.B., Sergeev, I.S.: Complexity of computation in finite fields. J. Math. Sci. **191**, 661–685 (2013). https://doi.org/10.1007/s10958-013-1350-5
4. Paulo, S.B., Voloch, J.F.: Efficient Computation of Roots in Finite Fields. Kluwer Academic Publishers, Amsterdam (2004)
5. Khabbazian, M., Gulliver, T., Bhargava, V.: Double point compression with applications to speeding up random point multiplication. IEEE Trans. Comput. **56**(3), 305–313 (2007)
6. Barreto, P.S.L.M., Kim, H.Y., Lynn, B., Scott, M.: Efficient algorithms for pairing-based cryptosystems. In: Yung, M. (ed.) CRYPTO 2002. LNCS, vol. 2442, pp. 354–369. Springer, Heidelberg (2002). https://doi.org/10.1007/3-540-45708-9_23
7. Duquesne, S., El Mrabet, N., Haloui, S., Rondepierre, F.: Choosing and generating parameters for pairing implementation on BN curves. Appl. Algebra Eng. Commun. Comput. **29**(2), 113–147 (2017). https://doi.org/10.1007/s00200-017-0334-y
8. Justus, B.: Point compression and coordinate recovery for Edwards curves over finite field. Analele University de Vest, Timisoara Seria Matematica Informatica LII **2**, 111–125 (2014)
9. Gashkov, S.B., Gashkov, I.B.: Fast algorithm of square rooting in some finite fields of odd characteristic. Mosc. Univ. Math. Bull. **73**(5), 176–181 (2018). https://doi.org/10.3103/S0027132218050029
10. King, B.: A point compression method for elliptic curves defined over $GF(2^n)$. In: Bao, F., Deng, R., Zhou, J. (eds.) PKC 2004. LNCS, vol. 2947, pp. 333–345. Springer, Heidelberg (2004). https://doi.org/10.1007/978-3-540-24632-9_24
11. Dudeanu, A., Oancea, G.R., Iftene, S.: An x-coordinate point compression method for elliptic curves over Fp. In: 12th International Symposium on Symbolic and Numeric Algorithms for Scientific Computing (2010)
12. Iyengar, V.S.: Efficient characteristic 3 Galois field operations for elliptic curve cryptographic applications. In: Proceedings of the 10th International Conference on Security and Cryptography (SECRYPT-2013), pp. 531–536 (2013). ISBN: 978-989-8565-73-0
13. Galbraith, S.D., Lin, X.: Computing pairings using x-coordinates only. Des. Codes Cryptogr. **50**, 305–324 (2009). https://doi.org/10.1007/s10623-008-9233-3
14. Faisal, Gazali, W.: An algorithm to find square root of quadratic residues over finite fields using primitive elements. In: 2nd International Conference on Computer Science and Computational Intelligence 2017, ICCSCI 2017, Bali, Indonesia, vol. 116, pp. 198–205, 13–14 October 2017. Procedia Computer Science (2017)
15. Brumley, B.B., Järvinen, K.U.: Fast point decompression for standard elliptic curves. In: Mjølsnes, S.F., Mauw, S., Katsikas, S.K. (eds.) EuroPKI 2008. LNCS, vol. 5057, pp. 134–149. Springer, Heidelberg (2008). https://doi.org/10.1007/978-3-540-69485-4_10
16. Koshelev, D.: New point compression method for elliptic Fq2-curves of j invariant 0. Finite Fields Th. App. **69**, 101774 (2021)
17. Zhang, Y., Li, Y., Chen, Q.: Fast asymptotic square root for two types of special Pentanomials. IEEE Access **7**, 50255–50264 (2019)
18. Adj, G., Rodriguez-Henriquez, F.: Square root computation over even extension fields. IEEE Trans. Comput. **63**, 2829–2841 (2012)

Author Index

Printed in the United States
by Baker & Taylor Publisher Services